AF895998

DISCARDED SELVES

Discarded Selves

OBSOLESCENCE IN THE AGE OF PRESENTISM

Gai Farchi

FORDHAM UNIVERSITY PRESS   NEW YORK 2027

Copyright © 2027 Fordham University Press

All rights reserved. No part of this publication may be reproduced, stored in a retrieval system, or transmitted in any form or by any means—electronic, mechanical, photocopy, recording, or any other—except for brief quotations in printed reviews, without the prior permission of the publisher.

Fordham University Press has no responsibility for the persistence or accuracy of URLs for external or third-party Internet websites referred to in this publication and does not guarantee that any content on such websites is, or will remain, accurate or appropriate.

Fordham University Press also publishes its books in a variety of electronic formats. Some content that appears in print may not be available in electronic books.

Visit us online at www.fordhampress.com.

For EU safety / GPSR concerns: Mare Nostrum Group B.V, Doelen 72, 4831 GR Breda, The Netherlands, gpsr@mare-nostrum.co.uk

Library of Congress Cataloging-in-Publication Data available online at https://catalog.loc.gov.

Printed in the United States of America

29 28 27   5 4 3 2 1

First edition

To Didi

Contents

DISCARDED SELVES

Introduction

A popular genre of YouTube videos titled "Kids React" captures children's responses to both long-past and recently obsolete phenomena. From early-2000s emo bands like My Chemical Romance to fax machines, from Missy Elliott to CD players, the children often confront these artifacts with bewilderment, struggling to make sense of technologies and cultural moments that no longer follow any recognizable logic. "What the —?" exclaims one appalled child in response to Missy Elliott's 2002 music video "Work It," while in another episode, a participant lifts the receiver of a fax machine's telephone, hoping somehow to receive a document.[1]

Unlike encounters with curated and monumental pasts, often infused with nostalgia, "Kids React" videos mobilize affects of uneasiness and discomfort. These are not simply revisitations of old Missy Elliott videos—they are recordings of how others respond to them. The dominant reactions are embarrassment, aversion, and cringe—the latter, in its contemporary usage, describing a visceral recoil from secondhand shame or awkwardness. Across these videos, the past is framed not through continuity but rupture. Their rhetorical force lies in the comedy of historical distance: The past is not merely quaint—it is absurd, inaccessible, and judged according to the moral and aesthetic norms of the present.

In *Minima Moralia*, Theodor Adorno, reflecting on Henrik Ibsen, argues that outdatedness is not simply a function of time but the "verdict of history."[2] As he puts it: "What was accomplished can be forgotten and preserved in the present. Only what failed is outdated—the broken promise of a new beginning."[3] While vintage cars are revered and vinyl records continue to thrive, obsolescence is less a matter of chronological distance than of cultural hygiene—a way the present sanitizes itself of unwanted residues.

This logic becomes particularly symptomatic of what François Hartog calls *presentism*, the temporal regime of our contemporary, in which the immediate now devours both historical reflection and future imagination.[4] Originally coined as a critical term to challenge ahistorical approaches to history by theorizing different "regimes of historicity," presentism designates a condition in which the present becomes the dominant horizon for both past and future. In this sense, presentism goes hand in hand with disposability—a logic that governs not only consumer goods but also the selves navigating short-lived attachments. In the cultural economy of presentism, the self is produced through gestures of rupture and disposal, while obsolescence signifies an unwanted remnant that lingers despite having been discarded. Within this regime, "Kids React" functions as a sorting device—determining what was absorbed into the present and what was cast off.

A striking subgenre of "Kids React" features children reacting to their own earlier appearances. In "Kids & Teens React to Kids React to Donald Trump (4 Years Later)," teenagers revisit their prior commentary on Trump's campaign.[5]

Lucas, recalling his early childhood endorsement, watches with his face in his hands: “Please don’t say it,” he begs his past self—knowing, of course, that he will. This phenomenon is not limited to children disavowing childish beliefs. The popular Canadian content creator KallMeKris posted a video titled “My Old Content Was So CRINGE . . . ,” admitting she is never comfortable with rewatching her own videos.[6] Similarly, the social media star Emma Chamberlain’s “REACTING TO MY OLD VIDEOS *cringe*” features her berating her younger self for a cherry-patch DIY on Vans shoes and her “painful” acting: “This hurts so fucking bad.”[7]

Why, actually, does it hurt so bad?

The obsolete is a historically and culturally produced lens through which the old and the aging are perceived as disruptive, negated, or doomed to irrelevance. “Obsolescence” comes from the Latin *obsol⊠scere*, meaning “to grow old or to wear out.”[8] While today the term is often associated with technological advancement, words, songs, and beliefs can become obsolete just as readily as commodities and gadgets. Obsolescence is a temporal dynamic. As Sarah Wasserman and Babette B. Tischleder have shown, its power lies in its paradox: The obsolete endures, yet it is suppressed.[9] Unlike disposable waste, the obsolete often retains its utility, accompanying the present as a remnant.[10]

Obsolescence offers a vantage point for understanding a culture that produces short-circuited fads and crazes. From the Ice Bucket Challenge (2014) to HQ Trivia (2014), fidget spinners (2017), Pokémon Go (2020), NFTs (2021), and “What were you like in the 90s?” videos (2026), each trend arrives already marked for expiration. Everything is swiftly exhausted and discarded, only to reappear in a new guise, as a shiny commodity, in the endless cycle of artificial novelty. This book reflects on what becomes of the residues we leave behind—material and cultural—as we move ever onward through this churn of perpetual replacement.

Digital culture has recently been understood not only as a regime that demands constant novelty but, paradoxically, as one that never truly erases its archive. In *Foreverism*, Grafton Tanner argues that contemporary cultures aspire to be evergreen by continually rebooting and recycling from an already exhausted archive.[11] Similarly, in *The End of Forgetting*, Kate Eichhorn describes the malaise of growing up in a digital era where nothing is ever truly deleted.[12] A focus on obsolescence reveals the fissure opened by these contradictory impulses: an ever-renewed resurrection of the past alongside a ceaseless archive that retains everything. The discarded is not erased; instead, under the relentless imperative for novelty, it persists as a remainder. This paradox—of irrelevance and persistence—defines obsolescence and positions it as a crucial lens through which to examine the contradictions of contemporary culture.

The central argument of this book is that obsolescence is not merely a condition imposed on objects or media but a temporal and affective logic internalized within the self. In a culture driven by disposability, subjectivity is increasingly shaped by the disowning of former attachments, affects, and formations of selfhood—what I call *discarded selves*. The book asks what happens when these discarded selves persist: when they resist being forgotten, erased, or recycled and instead insist on their obsolescence—time-stamped and saturated with the weight of their historical moment. It traces the narrative ways in which selves negotiate the imperative of disposability and the lingering of the obsolete—through encounters with outdated objects and cultural forms, from decluttering and ragpicking to the awkward intimacy of running into your ex.

In economies governed by rapid obsolescence and commodified transience, and amid a global climate crisis, we are called to think not only about what we consume but about what we discard: whether it is plastic or fleeting cultural moods, outdated media or discarded selves. To engage with the obsolete means assuming responsibility for the objects, attachments, and the selves we leave behind. And in doing so, we begin to sense the contours of time that arise not from seamless continuity but from the unresolved, the partial, and the no-longer-fitting.

The stakes of this argument lie in the possibility of cohabiting with otherness—not a radical or distant otherness but an intimate otherness embodied most concretely by our own discarded selves. The fissure in the fantasy of the present is what renders otherness thinkable—not only as a temporal beyond but as a disturbance inscribed within the very boundaries of selfhood. Cringe—the recurring affect in "Kids React" videos—is especially significant because it signals a form of identification through discomfort. As Melissa Dahl writes, cringe is "an unpleasant kind of self-recognition where you suddenly see yourself through someone else's eyes."[13] The shame is secondhand, but it is striking us because we can imagine ourselves in the scene. The structure of the videos—split between a past and present version of the same person and centered on a reaction of disavowal—makes visible the demand to detach from and discard earlier formations of the self through a marked temporal rupture. These videos reveal selves that were quickly formed and quickly abandoned now reappearing as intimate, familiar strangers.

In this respect, our encounters with discarded selves are inseparable from our attunement to otherness exhibited by aging and decay. Amid the rise of seductive, present-tense goods, the obsolete names what the present cannot assimilate: a forgotten Eurotrash hit, a now-unacceptable remark, or a teenage memory too awkward to reclaim. Yet it is precisely through these encounters with obsolete attachments that a different experience of time becomes possible. When the past is either neglected or recycled into the present, it is in the encounter with the obsolete—in that intimate moment of "no longer" otherness—that the temporal and material others of presentism come into view.

Adopting a method centered on close readings, *Discarded Selves* shows how the obsolete should be reexamined through narratives in which obsolescence functions as a dynamic force within the construction of narrated selfhood. A narrative approach to obsolescence involves tracing the cringe-inducing, undesired residues of the past that disrupt the contemporary drive to remain up to date or to produce ever "better versions" of ourselves, as though we, too, were technological objects keeping pace with the market. Rather than following linear narratives in which the old becomes the condition for the new, the obsolete unsettles storytelling through rupture, disruption, and misformation. I examine how narratives of decluttering negotiate the untimely residues of obsolete selves, for example, literary works that revisit past relationships or the familiar and unsettling experience of encountering one's own diary entries or neglected VCR cassettes.

To grasp the emerging temporal, material, and affective conditions of these stakes, I offer a brief genealogy of obsolescence—not as a strictly technological state but as a cultural and affective formation. The obsolete, as an orientation toward the past, is inseparable from the modern temporal regime. Across the chapters that follow, I examine both thinkers of modernism proper and post-1990s cultural texts to trace what transforms, develops, and becomes newly visible in our attunement to obsolescence. I address the ways in which the modernist tradition of the defunct and the obsolete—tied to the form of the reproducible commodity—intersects with these contemporary texts, revealing a dynamic reorientation in how obsolescence is confronted as a volatile remainder that disrupts the fantasy of seamless continuity.

Temporality

In 1932, the American real estate developer Bernard London proposed planned obsolescence as a solution to the Great Depression. Nostalgically recalling an era when "American people did not wait until the last possible bit of use had been extracted from every commodity," he advocated a radical cure for economic stagnation: the legally mandated acceleration of product obsolescence.[14] London envisioned a system in which the government would "assign a lease of life to shoes and homes and machines, to all products of manufacture, mining, and agriculture, when they are first created, and they would be sold and used within the term of their existence definitely known by the consumer."[15] Once this predetermined lifespan expired, goods would be legally declared "dead" and become subject to governmental control. In times of widespread unemployment, they would be destroyed, necessitating their replacement and thereby keeping the wheels of industry in constant motion.

London's proposal took on an eerie and unexpected afterlife. In the current age of disposable commodities, obsolescence has accelerated to the point of near-instantaneity—not through governmental decree but through economic and cultural tendencies. The overconsumption of disposable goods has become one of the defining crises of the Anthropocene, as evidenced by the depletion of energy resources and the ecological catastrophe of plastic waste inundating marine ecosystems.

Francis Fukuyama's *The End of History and the Last Man*, written shortly after the fall of the Berlin Wall, took a similar turn. In his book, which has accumulated fame and manifold known critics, Fukuyama celebrated the triumph of capitalism and free-market ideology, proclaiming it the final stage of ideological evolution.[16] Like London's vision, Fukuyama's thesis now appears irrelevant—not because capitalism has disappeared but because its unchallenged dominance has led to a global crisis Fukuyama did not foresee. Liberal capitalism remains the prevailing ideology, yet its unchecked expansion now threatens human survival amid climate catastrophe, a consequence of the very triumph Fukuyama once heralded.

What renders both London's and Fukuyama's pronouncements prone to obsolescence is their rhetorical double bind. On the one hand, they attempt to anticipate the unpredictable virtuality of the future, grasping at the unknowable. On the other hand, they actualize this future through the narrow perspective of their own historical moment. London's proposal for planned obsolescence was presented with a self-assurance that now appears irrelevant, unable to anticipate, from the perspective of economic depression, how obsolescence would become a cornerstone of postindustrial capitalism. Similarly, Fukuyama's thesis, as Jacques Derrida famously pointed out, is contingent upon actual historical conditions—such as the collapse of the Soviet Union—while simultaneously tying itself to the ideal of capitalist liberalism, an abstraction that resists actual manifestation.[17] It is in this sense that Derrida's hauntology serves as a counterpoint to Fukuyama's ontology: Whereas Fukuyama envisions the future from within the limits of his present—a "future-present" that forecloses historical openness—Derrida insists on the spectral presence of both past and future, both of them haunting the present in an untimely manner.

Unlike Derrida's specters, which haunt Fukuyama's vision by resisting ontological closure, the obsolete is entirely embedded in time. It is nothing but its own actuality—what once appeared forward-looking now reads, in hindsight, as misguided or cringeworthy. The obsolete is temporally closed—stamped in its age—and positions itself in rupture with the present. This is why, even though aspects of their visions have come true, the texts of London and Fukuyama "fail" retroactively. In a world of accelerated obsolescence, London's proposal now appears naïve, and even when capitalism seems invincible, the thesis of the "end of history" feels quaint. The specter remains open to the present, lingering as virtual potentiality. The obsolete, by contrast, is overdetermined by its pastness. It is this very actuality—its saturation with a now-disavowed past moment—that marks it for denial within a tightly curated present.

Precisely because the obsolete is so sealed in time, it bears the full weight of its moment. And in doing so, it offers a rare vantage on duration in a temporal regime that otherwise suppresses it. This echoes Walter Benjamin's contemplations on the Parisian arcades, which are imbued with a sense of outdatedness as the inevitable fate of every capitalist commodity.[18] The arcades, first established in the nineteenth century as glamorous spaces of desire and consumption, eventually became home to department stores, palm readers, and other dubious enterprises.[19] In Benjamin's dialectical thinking, capitalist progress is implicated in both the inception and demise of the arcades: Every present-tense promise of capitalist consumption is destined for substitution and displacement by the next object of desire. This process leaves behind the past in the form of obsolete spaces repurposed for uses far removed from their original intent.

The regime of presentism makes this temporality of the obsolete central like it has never been before. In this book, I use Hartog's notion of *presentism* to mark a shift from the modern, future-oriented imagination to an all-pervasive present. Presentism, I believe, is a fitting term to describe the entanglement between postindustrial acceleration and what has been called the "end of history." It captures the connective logic between the regime of disposability and that of the evergreen and time-proof—where things are at once fleeting and aspire to be immune to time. In *Regimes of Historicity*, Hartog explicitly cites Rem Koolhaas's notion of junkspace as an example of a presentist configuration of space that never ages.[20] Junkspaces, devoid of material and historical specificity, such as airports or shopping malls, are simultaneously the newest and the oldest. As Anna Kornbluh recently showed, the emerging culture of immediacy operates through a similar temporality, erasing the textures of mediation—those that are, in our context, time-stamped, delayed, or obsolete—in favor of seamless presentness.[21] This culture exemplifies presentism through an aspiration to immunity from its own becoming-past and, consequently, an inability to accommodate a future.

By this token, presentism is inherently bound up with disposability, even though the origins of disposability can be traced back to the early twentieth century. Gilles Slade notes that in the 1930s, the concept of disposability was initially introduced through the sale of paper goods marketed as disposable products.[22] However, this trend quickly expanded beyond simple paper items, evolving into a broader cultural ethos of "throwing away" that came to encompass a wide range of objects.[23] In this book, I refer to a critical juncture at which the logic of disposability—emerging in postwar Western capitalism—accelerates into a pervasive cultural condition of presentism, increasingly shaped by the development of digital media. This shift reflects a broader movement away from valuing durability and longevity toward privileging repetitive consumption, exemplified by the aesthetic and material preferability of plastic.

The logic of disposability embedded in plastic products,

for instance, catalyzes a rupture in temporal scales: The gap between the alchemical creation of plastic and its enduring indestructibility, spanning from a split-second miracle to millennia in the ocean, epitomizes the presentist paradoxes of consumption. All the while, just like the time-proof, a disposable plastic item strives for a kind of timelessness: Because its form and content are not easily datable (can one distinguish a plastic bag from 2002 from one made in 2022?), it effectively surrenders its place within historical narrative from the outset. It is in this sense that Gay Hawkins has associated the use of plastic with Hartog's definition of presentism.[24] The emergence of disposable plastics, which satisfy immediate needs but persist in the environment for centuries, epitomizes the presentist ethos. Perceiving disposability "as both a temporal and an iterative practice," the paradox of plastic—so durable yet meant for single use—can be explained only through the presentist fixation of our time.[25]

Whereas presentism demands time-proof content and recyclable selves, the obsolete is too heavy, too closed, and too committed to its moment. Trapped in the present they sought to universalize, London's and Fukuyama's projects become case studies of temporal overreach: the fantasy that time can be stabilized, directed, or concluded. In the age of presentism, this fantasy becomes systemic. The present no longer anticipates or mourns; it functions as a mechanism of sanitization where only present-tense, commodified content appears relevant. In presentism, the obsolete is no longer simply an aging thing but the residue of duration. It lingers precisely where the fantasy of the ever-new begins to break down, affecting not only cultural objects but selves, attachments, and narratives that no longer "fit" yet stubbornly persist.

This book proposes, then, an account of obsolescence after the end of history and within a regime of hyperplanned obsolescence. In this account, historical duration can be reintroduced through the very forms that appear to signal its disappearance. The seemingly irrelevant thesis on the end of history becomes, in retrospect, a glimpse into history's persistence, and the naïve vision of planned obsolescence becomes a threshold for understanding how obsolescence operates nearly a century later, as a time-bearing remainder within the seamless now.

Materiality

Obsolescence and disposability are conditions both temporal and material. To understand the material conditions of obsolescence in an era of presentism, we turn to a residential neighborhood of Austin, Texas, where, in the backyard of the artist Vince Hannemann, stands one of the city's most popular and quirky attractions: a three-story sculpture composed of discarded and defunct objects named the *Cathedral of Junk* (fig. 1). Hannemann, who personally schedules visits with curious tourists, regularly curates and alters his sculpture, which amalgamates junk from diverse sectors of consumer culture and various time periods.

In the *Cathedral of Junk*, CDs hang from the ceiling as metallic decor, while plastic and analog watches, bulky obsolete televisions, and nostalgic components of American automobiles are intricately entangled. Beyond its status as an anecdotal tourist attraction for selfie seekers, the *Cathedral of Junk* serves as a memorial to American consumer culture. Within its structure, chronological periods are compressed, with disparate objects performing new roles as art in their entangled state. This assemblage offers a complex commentary on consumption and obsolescence. Each assembled object, once an attractive commodity, appears here as materiality deprived of its aura. The artifacts, once imbued with novelty and promising present-tense engagement, are now relegated to a new context among other disenchanted presents. A 1990s television shares space with a 1970s car model, and a floppy disk finds its place in this graveyard alongside its replacement, the CD-ROM.

The *Cathedral of Junk* narrates the history of postwar consumption against a linear narrative of progress. It does not present a chronological flux of events where the new unremittingly substitutes the old, rendering it obsolete. Instead, it offers a compressed history in which the omnipresent feeling of the "no longer" is shared by objects from diverse temporal periods—a history consisting of a cycle of presents already imbued with their obsolescent fate. In this light, Benjamin's historical materialism offers a lens to understand obsolescence as a historicizing force, one beyond any particular commodity or promise. Famously articulated in his reflections on Paul Klee's *Angelus Novus*, Benjamin writes:

> A Klee painting named "Angelus Novus" shows an angel looking as though he is about to move away from something he is fixedly contemplating. His eyes are staring, his mouth is open, his wings are spread. This is how one pictures the angel of history. His face is turned toward the past. Where we perceive a chain of events, he sees one single catastrophe which keeps piling wreckage upon wreckage and hurls it in front of his feet. The angel would like to stay, awaken the dead, and make whole what has been smashed. But a storm is blowing from Paradise; it has got caught in his wings with such violence that the angel can no longer close them. This storm irresistibly propels him into the future to which his back is turned, while the pile of debris before him grows skyward. This storm is what we call progress.[26]

Benjamin's angel of history, caught in the wind of progress, perceives the past not as a "chain of events" but as "one single catastrophe." To its eyes, the past appears not as a chronological and progressive narrative of novelty replacing an outdated past but as a single, compressed layer of debris. While the *Cathedral of Junk* is aesthetically curated and certainly cannot be construed as a mere pile of debris, it performs for the beholder a similar compression of temporality and materiality. Here, history is perceived from the perspective of the leftover, the outdated, and the obsolete. It places before our eyes the anticipated fate of every present and alluring promise under capitalism. The cathedral's representation challenges linear conceptions of progress, instead presenting a palimpsest of consumer culture where past and present coexist in a state of perpetual obsolescence.

Something quite different happens in the artworks of Tim Noble and Sue Webster. The London-based artists assembled heaps of residue, including discarded toilet paper, plastic cups, and waste bearing the unmistakable marks of

Figure 1. Vince Hanneman, *Cathedral of Junk*. Photo by Didi Atsmon.

brands like McDonald's and Coca-Cola, and transformed them into sculptures that cast meaningful shadows. In one piece, a pile of trash, when exposed to light, reveals the shadow of two people sitting back to back, enjoying a cigarette and a glass of wine (fig. 2). In another, the shadow depicts two lovers embracing, one leaning over the other.

Figure 2. Noble and Webster, *Dirty White Trash (with Gulls)*, 1998. © 2026 Tim Noble and Sue Webster. All Rights Reserved, DACS Images. Photographer: Andy Keates.

Without the need for overly intricate interpretation, these sculptures expose the romantic image operating as a façade, masking the reality of the rubble as its immediate consequence. While Noble and Webster's sculptures critique the negative overproduction inherent in disposable consumption, this reading only scratches the surface of their work. What their sculptures truly emphasize is the vast and irreconcilable gap between two regimes: the regime of consumption and the regime of its residues. The rubbish in Noble and Webster's sculptures is entirely useless—its function exhausted after a single use. The romantic shadows produced by the heaps highlight this divide, illustrating how the allure of consumption conceals the ultimate destiny of waste. In their work, the obsolete is not present; instead, disposability reigns, creating a stark temporal contrast between the fleeting allure of the commodity and the permanence of its discarded remnants.

The regime of disposability both draws on and complicates previous understandings of residual objects. Michael Thompson's *Rubbish Theory*, for example, categorized commodities into two forms: the transient (whose value decreases over time) and the durable (whose value increases over time), with rubbish serving as the essential zero-degree state from which an object can transition between these categories through cycles of cultural and economic exchange.[27] In this sense, what Noble and Webster's sculptures illuminate is the growing disconnection between the realms of rubbish and the commodity. Precisely because the disposable is immediately rubbish, it cannot pass through a stage of obsolescence; it is useless from the outset and rarely—if ever—recovers value.

The regime of disposability is also the regime of recyclability. The only way for an object to pass into the category of rubbish and acquire value again is at the price of losing its identity as an object. Plastic, in particular, embodies this paradox, as it is created without any fixed identity, designed to be remade rather than reused. The gap between the romantic shadows and the heaps of rubbish performs recyclability as a temporal tendency: The new is immediately exhausted, stripped of value, and reintroduced as new, appearing within the commodity cycle without bearing any trace of time or history. In a culture dependent on repetitive consumption, recyclability allows us to bypass the phase of pastness—of obsolescence—instead of embracing reuse and reducing consumption.

Günther Anders's life work *The Obsolescence of the Human* (*Die Antiquiertheit des Menschen*) offers a profound anticipatory vision of the paradigm shift regarding obsolescence. Writing in 1958, Anders already recognized that postwar commodities were "born to die," forming an eternal cycle of novelty in which production and destruction no longer stand in opposition but become integral to the same mechanism.[28] The postindustrial system continuously reproduces and destroys, only to reproduce again. Here, Anders offers his own alternative vision of Benjamin's *Angelus Novus*, one resonating with Noble and Webster's heap much more than the *Cathedral of Junk*. In a world where both past and future are dismissed, the angel's gaze no longer fixes upon the wreckage of history but becomes transfixed by the present moment.[29] This fixation, incapable of perceiving the past as debris, reverses the historical insight that Benjamin ascribes to Klee's angel. Fixated solely on the present, ahistorical amnesia is what the angel sees.

The two heaps, as the two angels, mark not a sharp rupture but an acceleration of the same logic: The promptly obsolete consumer item becomes, in Noble and Webster, disposable and valueless from the outset. Yet the objects in the *Cathedral of Junk* bear enough historical weight to be mourned and resalvaged. In contrast, Noble and Webster's sculptures negate any form of encounter with the past, remaining fixated on immediate consumption in the present. Under conditions of disposability and recyclability, the obsolete therefore maintains its identity and form—insisting on its historical specificity and resisting the elasticity of the recyclable commodity. As a liminal and ephemeral form, the obsolete evades the devouring force of presentism, appearing awkward and distant despite mechanisms of recycling. This recycling is at times material (the commodity is transformed into another shape) but more intensely just symbolic, as past fads tend to be repackaged as-is as new, promising commodities.

Affect

Mourning, nostalgia, and cringe are all possible affective contours in our encounters with obsolete things. Yet these affects, too, have a dynamic and uneven history. Obsolescence co-emerges as the shadow of modernity's temporality of progress, fissuring the present while aiming to capture it. The etymological roots of modernity in *modo* (meaning "just now") reveal a paradox: Modernity's very essence engenders a diachronic rupture, instantly dividing time into "now" and "no longer." Obsolescence as a modern structure of feeling, one inseparable from the emergence of the reproducible commodity, is central to canonical modernist thought—particularly, as we have seen, in Benjamin's historical materialism.

If, for Benjamin, modernity is bound to the decline of the aura—that is, the erosion of original presence—then obsolescence emerges as a distinctly modern phenomenon insofar as only the reproducible can anticipate its own fading and replacement by the next novelty.[30] In his poem "The Swan"

("Le cygne") from 1859, Charles Baudelaire, considered by Benjamin the poet embodying these modern transitions, describes an emerging feeling of exile within time. The poem, dedicated to the exiled Victor Hugo, laments the considerable change in Paris, which was rebuilt under the regime of Napoleon III in a systematic effort led by Baron Haussmann:

> Paris may change, but in my melancholy mood
> Nothing has budged!
> New palaces, blocks, scaffoldings,
> Old neighbourhoods, are allegorical for me,
> And my dear memories are heavier than stone.[31]

Baudelaire's poem revolves around the image of a swan that has escaped its cage but longs for water, finding only dry pavement to walk on. The swan, like Baudelaire himself, is exiled not in space but in time. Baudelaire's melancholic lamentation of the changing Paris is singular and prescient in its historical context. In modernity, and amid industrial capitalism, time is accelerated, engendering a feeling of untimeliness, of a longing for a fleeting moment so easily missed. Baudelaire, who was always keen on aligning himself with the wretched and the damned of the city, extends his sympathy to the outdatedness of old quarters, heavy under the burden of old memories. "The Swan" emerges as a quintessential manifestation of *spleen*, the insidious form of melancholy that permeates Baudelaire's poetry. The poem captures the modern condition as inherently belated and exiled, perpetually not-at-home and not-on-time.

Marshall Berman's dictum—"To be modern is to be part of a universe in which, as Marx said, 'All that is solid melts into air'"—encapsulates the perpetual state of unremitting ephemerality and the insatiable search for anchors.[32] In this respect, Baudelaire's spleen parallels the modern transformation of nostalgia from a curable disease—treated in early modern times with leeches and opium—to a condition that defines the modern age, a pervasive cultural malaise construed as the inevitable byproduct of progress.[33] "The Swan" is equally an exemplar of the *post-festum* ("after the feast") tendency that Gerhard Richter termed *Afterness*, a temporality depicting the modern subject as always late in capturing the "right" time.[34] In modernity, the desire to experience the present paradoxically engenders a pervasive sense of belatedness—as if one has arrived at a party after its conclusion.

By the same token, Baudelaire positions the dated and the stamped—clear mirrors of the outdated and the obsolete—not as disposable traits of art and creation but as arguably their most important quality. In "The Painter of Modern Life," he defines modernity as "the ephemeral, the fugitive, the contingent, the half of art whose other half is the eternal and the immutable."[35] His definition grasps modernity as the stamp of time itself—the expression, the smile, and all the other aesthetic carriages of an age. For Baudelaire, any attempt to eliminate this transitory nature results in emptiness and abstraction. He asserts that "almost all our originality comes from the seal which Time imprints on our sensations."[36]

In much the same way, the obsolete stands as the residue of modernity's relentless pursuit of progress. Whether an object, an expression, or a cultural phenomenon, obsolescence is bound to an accelerated sense of irrevocable change—where ideals, hopes, and promises hinge on the fleeting yet carry an essence inaccessible by any other means. Baudelaire takes a seemingly timeless ideal like beauty—traditionally considered beyond the contingent—and imbues it with two paradoxical components. One is "eternal and invariable"; the other consists of circumstantial elements: "the age, its fashions, its morals, its emotions."[37] For Baudelaire, both are indispensable. If beauty is a divine cake—his own metaphor—the eternal element would be indigestible without the temporal, fleeting ingredient: the teasing, ephemeral coating. Beauty, as illustrated in his poem "To a Passerby" ("À une passante"), is inextricably bound to the fleeting presence of the woman passing on the street.[38] Yet, as the poem suggests, the ideal's transience is so brief that we inevitably arrive too late—the passerby has already vanished, the moment already lost.

Under this temporal regime, the commodity becomes at once the rupture in presence and its compensation; the souvenir, for example, carries within it the death of the experience—but it is also a means to possess this very experience, which would otherwise flee into oblivion.[39] The melancholic, however, resists this allegorical substitution. Melancholy, which echoes Baudelaire's spleen, marks an inability to let go. Baudelaire cannot accept ephemerality because he clings to the fleeting object—in his case, pre-Haussmannian Paris. This interplay finds its psychoanalytic formation in Freud's "Mourning and Melancholia," where he distinguishes between normative mourning, in which libidinal attachments are gradually displaced, and melancholia, in which they are turned inward and incorporated rather than relinquished.[40]

Something different happens with affects such as cringe and aversion, which do not emerge from excessive attachment but from its collapse. They belong to a cultural logic in which melancholia is less permitted to unfold, because the object—whether thing or self—is meant to be instantly replaceable. This, of course, resonates with the nature of the disposable item itself: Unlike the objects in the *Cathedral of Junk*, which retain enough temporal thickness to invite mourning or nostalgia, the waste in Noble and Webster's work is so stripped of duration that it forecloses both.

Under the imperative of disposability, the persistence of

the obsolete—bearing the weight of its historical moment—registers as more scandalous than ever, provoking affective abjection. Like Julia Kristeva's example of skin on the surface of warm milk—something both internal but viscerally rejected—the past self is not incorporated but expelled ("I expel *myself*, I spit *myself* out"), a gesture that, as Sara Ahmed notes in her discussion of shame, reflects the self's impulse to turn away from itself in disgust while it has "nowhere to turn."[41] The discarded self thus turns to a form of complete disavowal, reconstituted through acts of self-disposal in a loop of accelerated obsolescence.

Unlike the modernist spleen, the presentist self has little to hold onto, and therefore it turns not to melancholic attachment but to instant disavowal. Mourning becomes fast and hygienic, structured around substitution and immediate compensation; the lost object is not grieved but overwritten by its update. This creates an affective regime tethered to consumption but increasingly totalizing: a world of ephemeral attachments, where the imperative is smooth disposal—no lingering and no strings attached. Throughout this book, I explore not only the discomfort of encountering discarded selves but also the varied strategies through which individuals negotiate this imperative—through self-curatorial practices such as collecting or through the reclamation of slow, visible aging. In a culture where decay, ruin, and old age are increasingly invisible—folded into either youth or death, alluring plastic or total waste—such gestures refuse the demand for seamless renewal, rendering the obsolete a space of temporal force and potential refuge.

Otherness

Discarded selves signify both a malaise and a potential. When the present enacts a temporal hygiene against untimely residues, obsolescence is not merely the fate of objects but a structure of subjective dispossession. The fact that so-called cringe influencers are already alienated from their own past selves opens a potential for solidarity through shared dispossession: If we are all so promptly estranged from our discarded selves, then each encounter with our internal otherness becomes a step toward encountering otherness more broadly.

One of the book's central examples of how otherness is negotiated appears in the relation between obsolete human and nonhuman forms. In a culture where the logic of disposability applies equally to people and things—casting aside the outmoded person no less than the outdated object—obsolescence offers a shared sanctuary. In practices such as ragpicking, hoarding, collecting, and childhood play, obsolescence appears not as a problem to be solved but as a space for reconfiguring relations beyond the subject-object divide.

This thinking unfolds within the broader eclipse of production by consumption. Presentism matches the regime of simulacra, obscuring the materiality of labor and its often exploitative nature behind the circulation of ever-new commodities. As Bill Brown suggests, London's call for planned obsolescence sought to impose a mortality on objects in order to affirm the human right to work—a logic that now appears itself obsolescent, as labor becomes increasingly obscured by consumption.[42] Throughout the book, I use the term *postindustrial* to describe a material condition—emerging in the postwar period and intersecting with late capitalism—in which immateriality and simulacra have culturally displaced the visible structures of industrial production. Yet it is important to remember that the disappearance of labor's material traces and the recurrent rendering of labor itself as obsolete are part of the violence that the category of obsolescence seeks to expose and demystify.

Brown's reflection on London underscores the shared mortality of humans and objects—a dynamic that remains evident today, as disposability extends across bodies, species, and forms. A society built on disposability inevitably turns this principle upon itself, subjecting humans to the same cycles of replacement that govern commodities. Celebrities, friendships, and romantic attachments all follow trajectories of rise and decline within a cultural economy where both persons and things are commodified and rendered obsolete. Anything consumed can become obsolete: Obsolescence, as both a temporal and material condition, respects no boundaries between human and nonhuman forms. Amid the climate crisis, which continues to uphold the divide between natures and cultures, humans and nonhumans, a critique of obsolescence invites us to see the human as one interdependent form within a shared economy of decay and renewal.

Whether it manifests as an object encapsulating memories or as a thing resisting disposal, obsolescence disrupts the traditional roles of subject and object. Under this framework, the obsolete object, to use Brown's terms once again, becomes a *thing* rather than merely an object. According to Brown, *thingness* conveys an expressive and excessive quality that exceeds the confines of objecthood, insofar as objecthood presupposes a subject that exerts its influence upon the object.[43] In addition, obsolete objects often appear not as objects but as "stuff," a category that, as Maurizia Boscagli defined it, is reserved for things that have shed their glamour yet resist being cast aside.[44]

While my analysis extends beyond material objects, the main field I engage with is material cultural studies, including Brown's "Thing Theory" and later works by scholars such as Boscagli, Tischleder, Wasserman, and Rebecca Falkoff.[45] Within literary studies, Francesco Orlando's classic work *Obsolete Objects in the Literary Imagination* has shown how Western literature, up to the twentieth century, has absorbed and reimagined obsolescence within cultural and literary consciousness.[46] More recently, Tischleder and Wasserman's edited volume *Cultures of Obsolescence* has examined obsolescence across its various manifestations in literature and art, primarily within the American context, with a significant focus on its role in the digital sphere.[47] Challenging the immaterial promise of digitality, the collection underscores the enduring presence not only of obsolete objects but of obsolescence as a persistent paradigm.

This book intervenes in material culture studies by rethinking obsolescence not merely as the fate of things but as a temporal and affective structure that governs subjectivity—particularly under the regime of presentism and disposability. Central to this intervention is the form of subjective dispossession that emerges across the book's case studies, which trace not only the aesthetics but also the ethical dimension of encountering discarded selves. The book unfolds in three pairs of chapters, each forming a conceptual dyad. Yet each chapter, in its own right, examines a different encounter in which the obsolete is negotiated against the imperative to dispose and move on, illuminating the narrative structures through which temporal disjunctions—what remains out of sync—shape how selves and cultural forms are framed, disavowed, or reclaimed.

The first chapter, "This Moment Is Going to Be a Memory," juxtaposes the modern fascination with déjà vu and the concept of *dès vu*, which *The Dictionary of Obscure Sorrows* defines as the awareness that the present moment will inevitably become a memory. In dès vu, the present is so promptly consumed that its value—the anticipated joy of remembering—is extracted even as the moment unfolds. This phenomenon exemplifies a culture in which time itself becomes disposable, instantly consumed and exhausted.

However, through a comparative analysis of Henri Bergson's interpretation of déjà vu and an examination of diary writing in Patrick Modiano's *The Black Notebook* alongside the series *The Mortified Podcast*, this chapter argues that confronting an obsolete version of oneself opens the possibility for an impersonal form of remembrance.

Building on this understanding of memory, the second chapter—"Nonimages"—examines the dès vu image in contrast to the stock photograph, which aspires to be timeproof. It argues that while the stock image aims to offer a stable and universal representation, it ultimately enables performances of identity that never fully align with their intended ideals, producing a form of unintentional camp. This analysis reveals how the generic photograph shifts from an ostensibly neutral, amnesiac image into a culturally charged medium through which identities and obsolete cultural forms are continuously negotiated—mirroring the performative logic of the presentist self.

Chapter 3, "Old Flames," examines case studies such as Orhan Pamuk's *The Museum of Innocence* and the cult films *High Fidelity* (2000) and *Eternal Sunshine of the Spotless Mind* (2004) to explore the untimeliness and obsolescence inherent in fleeting romantic encounters—epitomized by the infamous "morning after," which marks the immediate and awkward obsolescence of the discarded partner. By aligning the practice of collecting with the desire to preserve and mourn these transient experiences, the chapter illustrates how love—now more mediated and objectified than ever—is controlled and negotiated through various forms of collecting, which suspend the obsolescence of the romantic encounter within a self-curated narrative.

The fourth chapter, "Postindustrial Ragpicking," deepens the engagement with material obsolescence by turning to the practice of ragpicking, recognizing its capacity for transformation and reappropriation within the realm of postindustrial capitalism. By engaging closely with Annie Ernaux's oeuvre alongside documentaries depicting present-day New York City, this chapter examines how writing navigates the boundaries between the private and the public, reclaiming the residues of postindustrial junkspaces while opening the self to the impersonal registers of shared experience.

In Chapter 5, "Childish Profanations," dedicated to narratives of decluttering and the profanation of commodities, I examine the pathologization of uneconomic attachments to obsolete items. The chapter explores why and how contemporary narratives of decluttering in self-help and psychoanalytic literature are perceived as challenges to the realm of consumption and frame certain forms of "bad consumption," such as compulsive hoarding, as markers of infantile selfhood. The attachment of individuals who clutter to their obsolete possessions highlights a form of resistance to a culture that values the ability to dispose of things without emotional ties—a culture that symbolically celebrates the act of discarding commodities in anticipation of continuous consumption.

Chapter 6, "Aged Unwell," continues to explore obsolescence through the lens of the marginalized and pathologized, now shifting focus to the experience of aging. Delving into Michel Houellebecq's portrayal of aging, white, middle-class protagonists grappling with physical and cultural decline in *The Map and the Territory* and *Serotonin*, it examines obsolescence from the standpoint of those who find themselves lonely and disillusioned—white, old men dispossessed of the world they once inhabited. The chapter explores the post-festum temporality that Houellebecq assigns to both humans and objects under presentism, emphasizing how individuals, much like commodities, are subject to cycles of consumption, recycling, and eventual disposal.

The final chapter, "Better to Burn Out Than to Fade Away," explores both personal and impersonal forms of preservation over time, emphasizing the role of historically situated musical repetition in shaping future musical virtualities. Through the lens of Deleuzian thinking of time and repetition, it examines the logic behind an obsolete music style and the enduring, endlessly repeated hit, as well as recent AI-generated attempts to produce "new" songs for bands that no longer exist, such as Nirvana's "Drowned in the Sun." Drawing on fragments from Kurt Cobain's writings—and positioning itself against the line from his suicide note "It's better to burn out than to fade away"—the chapter rethinks repetition within and beyond the self not as a mere recycling of an exhausted state but as a generative force of creation.

The concluding Envoi weaves these narratives together toward a meditation on intimate otherness. I reflect on how our encounters with obsolescence involve an ethical stance not toward radical alterity but toward a more proximate otherness provoked by the discarded versions of ourselves. Ritualizing these encounters becomes a way of taking responsibility for what we leave behind in a culture defined by disposability, in which residues are doomed to persist unaccounted for, afar from visibility.

1
This Moment Is Going to Be a Memory

John Koenig's *The Dictionary of Obscure Sorrows*, a collection of neologisms for timely but unnamed emotions, offers an illustration of contemporary disposable approach to time in its definition of the term *dès vu*. Unlike the familiar déjà vu (French for "already seen"), dès vu ("seen from now on") denotes "the awareness that this moment will become a memory."[1] Dès vu is, therefore, the experience of the present as reminiscence, akin to a self-made time capsule; it is a moment where one "can almost feel the presence" of a future self, looking back in reflection.[2] For Koenig, the dès vu, not unlike the déjà vu, is an experience of self-doubling. He writes: "You are two people, separated by an ocean of time. Part of you bursting to talk about what you saw. Part of you longing to tell you what it all means."[3] This bifurcation of the self into present and future entities establishes an economy of remembrance, creating debts and credits across temporal dimensions.

The act of memorializing the present subordinates the moment to personal possession, preventing it from passing unvalued or unremembered. Like a speculative investment, the present self pays homage to the future self through the immediate acquisition of experiences. Conversely, the future self becomes indebted to the past self, obligated to find value in these preserved memories. This future self may "cringe and laugh, or brim with pride, aching to return."[4] However, many memories so eagerly collected would appear trivial or meaningless from our current vantage point, highlighting the complex interplay between our past, present, and future selves in this economy of reminiscence. The present, perceived as a memory, is so urgently consumed that its value, the rememberable joy of the present moment, is extracted and disposed of as this moment unfolds.

The dès vu permeates contemporary culture, from social media platforms centered on personal archiving to the popularity of services like Legacy Boxes, which digitize old home movies and pictures. The digitization and cloud storage of memory-archives render reminiscence readily available: Every Instagram post, in this sense, is dramatized and lived with an awareness of its future dissemination. By no coincidence, for Hartog, the making-event of the present is emblematic of presentism, where events can be constantly mediatized, produced, and consumed in an accelerating movement that seeks to view the present, "in the very moment of its occurrence," as already past.[5] The dès vu is a defining experience for a culture in which time itself becomes disposable and immediately exhausted.

This chapter explores how memory is shaped at the intersection of disposability and obsolescence, revealing their entangled logics within the mnemonic mechanism. Through the case study of the dès vu, it shows how an economy of disposability is internalized, producing a mechanism of mnemonic exhaustion and self-obsolescence. All the while, moments swiftly registered and discarded resist erasure and persist through our encounters with obsolete media. To trace this connection, I begin by linking dès vu to modernist conceptions of reminiscence and déjà vu in the works of Marcel Proust and Henri Bergson, followed by its entanglements with the contemporary author Patrick Modiano. With an understanding of dès vu as intertwined with the accelerated inscription of memory onto external technologies—destined for their own obsolescence—I explore particular interactions with forgotten or neglected VHS tapes in the performance show *Greetings from the Past.*

My interpretation of dès vu, as opposed to the familiar déjà vu, examines it in relation to a transformation of the economy of remembrance introduced by a disposable orientation to time itself. Dès vu is emblematic of the capitalism of disposables, representing the paradoxical desire to consume the present while simultaneously accelerating its obsolescence. However, rather than romanticizing the loss of an ostensibly authentic and immediate present, I see in dès vu the potential to reconsider the parameters of selfhood within a cycle of perpetually disposable presents. As Koenig suggested, the dès vu doubles the self by the very act of capturing a present that has already vanished. Yet this recurrent movement of self-estrangement conditions the self as a discarded "other," since the memorialized present always becomes the possession of the previous, now estranged self. From this threshold, the economy of remembrance easily subverts its own desire for the immediate possession of time, allowing for the emergence of impersonal forms of memory.

Memories Without Aura

The dès vu is a neologism derived from déjà vu, but their connection transcends linguistics. Dès vu represents a contemporary manipulation of the modernist déjà vu: the dès vu desperate and obsessive, the déjà vu spontaneous and involuntary. In the modernist fascination with involuntary memory, Marcel Proust stands as an unavoidable milestone. The most famous instance of involuntary memory in *In Search of Lost Time* (*À la recherche du temps perdu*) depicts the resurgence of memories of Combray, the town where the narrator spent fragmented periods of his childhood. In the novel's overture, the taste of a petite madeleine soaked in tea triggers the Combray memory, marking a unity of present and past. "Combray, town and gardens alike," rises from the madeleine, salvaging from oblivion the same tea-soaked cakes given to the narrator in childhood by his aunt Léonie.[6] Though not entirely involuntary (the narrator deliberately dips his madeleine in tea multiple times), this unity of present and past triumphantly carries the unity of the reminiscent self: "this new sensation having had the effect, which love has, of filling me with a precious essence; or rather this essence was not in me, it *was* me."[7]

The madeleine moment, along with other involuntary resurrections mentioned in Proust's work—such as the memory of Venice's uneven paving stones—resurfaces in the final sections of *À la recherche* to celebrate involuntary memory as a means of uniting the self outside of time:

> The truth surely was that the being within me which had enjoyed these impressions had enjoyed them because they had in them something that was common to a day long past and to the present, because in some way they were extra-temporal, and this being made its appearance only when, through one of these identifications of the present with the past, it was likely to find itself in the one and only medium in which it could exist and enjoy the essence of things, that is to say: outside time. This explained

> why it was that my anxiety on the subject of my death had ceased at the moment when I had unconsciously recognized the taste of the little madeleine, since the being which at that moment I had been was an extra-temporal being and therefore unalarmed by the vicissitudes of the future.[8]

Proust elevates spontaneous recollection in the form of involuntary memory, celebrating it as genuine remembrance, in contrast to the mechanical, voluntary memory of the intellect. Rather than a present that mourns its own becoming-past, involuntary memory soothes any "vicissitudes of the future," among them one central vicissitude, mortality. The extratemporal nature of involuntary memory also elevates the narrator beyond his mortal existence actualized in time. If the memory of Combray is extratemporal, it is supposedly independent of aging and therefore of obsolescence.

For Benjamin, involuntary memory is closely tied to the concept of aura, as it captures the past that was missed because of the accelerating repetition of reproducible events.[9] This form of memory reclaims a past that had been anesthetized in response to the overwhelming stimuli of modernity, restoring it as the auratic form of experience.[10] Yet something quite different happens in dès vu. While involuntary memory is genuine and auratic, the voluntary actualization of memory in dès vu assumes reproducibility and, ultimately, disposability.

Although Proust is frequently discussed in relation to Bergson's notion of the indefinite past (*passé indéfini*), Bergson's interpretation of false recognition (*fausse reconnaissance*)—synonymous for him with déjà vu—completes the echo of Proust's madeleine moment. Bergson suggests that every present moment is doubled by perception and memory: perception as the apparent "first" encounter with the present and simultaneously as an inscription of this present into the virtual register of memory.[11] Contrary to the belief that memory is a diluted form of perception (where perception is the "first" or "immediate" experience and memory merely its representation), both perception and memory operate at the very same time. One is directed toward the future and the other toward the past.

Bergson defines déjà vu as an unintended fusion of the registers of memory and perception. Instead of directing ourselves toward the future through perception, déjà vu offers a glimpse into the other register's workings—the ongoing inscription of the present as the past. This "glitch" in the process makes us feel as though we have experienced a certain situation before, revealing the present's inscription as a past event rather than directing our actions toward the future. In contrast to Proustian involuntary memory, where the self achieves unity beyond temporal constraints, déjà vu therefore creates a division within the self into two,

> one of which, conscious of its liberty, erects itself into an independent spectator of a scene which the other seems to be playing in a mechanical way. But this duplication does not go through to the end. It is rather an oscillation between two standpoints from which one views oneself, a going and coming of the mind between perception which is only perception and perception duplicated with memory.[12]

Bergson uses an economical logic to define the perception and memory registers. The memory register, which inscribes the present's transformation into the past, is virtual rather than actual. This register is not regularly actualized in time; we do not routinely see the present becoming the past. Instead, the inscription of the present as past is preserved in virtuality as indefinite memory, actualizing only when consciousness summons it, as in reminiscence. If this memory register were to actualize in time, we would need to chronologically revisit every memory to recollect a specific moment from the past. Therefore, for Bergson, personal recollections are "essentially fugitive," materializing by chance to align with bodily determination.[13] The memory content of consciousness is summoned to actuality only in "extraordinary cases," operating on a utilitarian logic: "The past only reappears to consciousness insofar as it can aid us in understanding the present and foreseeing the future."[14] Déjà vu presents a past that has no role, ostensibly, in the understanding of the future: It is the emergence of the memory register as a mistake and therefore exists outside this Bergsonian mnemonic economy.

In contrast, dès vu imposes a desire for consumption and exhaustion within the economy of memory. To ensure that the moment is remembered, it makes the memory register actual and therefore consumable, immediately extracting from the present its potential for future remembrance or reflection. When I frame the present moment as a memory and impose the lens of the memory register upon it, I transform it from virtuality to actuality. In dès vu, the desire to archive and nostalgically frame the present from its inception lacks the fugitive, chance encounter characteristic of déjà vu or involuntary memory. Instead, dès vu involves an excessively voluntary memory, so excessive that it is experiencing the present as if it were already a memory.

Following the logic of disposability, the immediate consumption of the present as actuality renders it obsolete from the start. In dès vu, consumption equates to actualization: The present is experienced as a memory along a chronological timeline, with the intent to frame, capture, and control it. However, once remembrance duplicates the self within actuality, rather than unifying it beyond temporal constraints, the credit intended for a future self inevitably becomes obsolete currency, destined to be discarded. As we will see, the drive to actualize and consume time contradicts itself by giving rise to an impersonal form of memory—one that is so immediately captured and disposed of that it cannot be possessed by any singular entity.

Note to Self

When we recognize that "this present moment is going to be a memory," we engage with time in a way that is intertwined not only with consumption but also with reproducibility. We have seen how the dès vu represents a memory without aura and that its voluntary nature signals the decline of the aura it seeks to compensate for. The notion that the fleeting moment can be archived, preserved, and deemed valuable in the future ("Do you remember when … ?") assumes its reproducibility in the future, and the culture of dès vu exemplifies this: The smartphone camera attempts to archive every moment, anticipating its future worth as a memory. Precisely because this memory is voluntary and reproducible from the outset, it becomes immediately obsolete, destined to clutter the smartphone's storage alongside all the other accumulated dès vu moments.

This disposability accelerates the duplication of selfhood. As we frame the present as a memory, we capture it as though through the lens of a camera, extracting it from the continuous flow of time. This act of capturing and consuming the moment instantly estranges us from it: The dès vu moment is already "past" us and thus seems to belong to someone quite different from us. This disposable estrangement introduces a new way to perceive the possession and dispossession of our memories. When memories are captured voluntarily, lingering in obsolescence and signifying alienation and distance from the aspirations of our current selves, we practice our nonexistence.

A primary example is found in Patrick Modiano's novella *The Black Notebook* (*L'herbe des nuits*), where a dès vu feeling is omnipresent. The narrative, like much of Modiano's oeuvre, is delivered by an uncanny double of Modiano himself, this time named Jean, who is compulsively driven to trace past events and relive his memories. In this story, traces from Jean's past are inscribed in a notebook he used in his twenties—a time marked by a love affair with a mysterious student named Dannie and the encounters with her even more enigmatic friends in Paris's Rive Gauche. The narrator attempts to sort through past memories that echo the assassination of Mehdi Ben Barka in 1965. Although the opaque notebook cannot provide a clear recollection of memories, its traces serve as the only proof of a seemingly lived past: "No, it wasn't a dream. The proof is that I still have this black notebook full of jottings."[15] The notebook resists simple classification as either a "private journal" or "fragments of memoir" and contains a "succession of names, phone numbers, appointments, and also short texts that might have something to do with literature."[16]

However, Jean insists on piecing together his past from these details. Jean's notebook carries a sense of debt to his future self, coupled with the anxiety that the elusive Dannie might vanish from his memory without this written proof of her existence. As Jean reads the notebook, he confronts his present inability to decipher a code he had once established—a record of a time he himself lived. The notebook immediately creates a rift between his present and past selves. Even the notes he took in his twenties about others' experiences, like references to distant historical events, are more comprehensible to him than the cryptic notes about his own life within the notebook.[17] Jean admits:

> But I read certain phrases, certain names, certain indications, and it seems to me I was sending out coded signals to the future. Yes, it's as if I wanted to leave clues, in black and white, that would help me clarify at some later date what I'd been living through at the time without really understanding it. Signals keyed blindly, in total confusion. And I'd have to wait years and years before I could decipher them.[18]

This passage exemplifies an untimeliness inherent in the reminiscent self, now confronting its own temporal dispersion. As in other works by Modiano, such as *Dora Bruder*, this displacement in time is mapped onto the streets of Paris. Jean, in a deliberate and voluntary manner, wanders through these streets with his notebook, only to discover that nothing remains as it once was. He revisits the 66, a twenty-four-hour café where he spent many evenings, and orders a Cointreau "in the memory of Dannie."[19] The bartender, who is about twenty-five and seems perplexed by Jean's questions, admits that they no longer stay open late.[20] Later, the neighborhood where Jean and Dannie once walked together feels "foreign" and "indifferent."[21] Not only is Jean unable to decipher his own notes, but those notes also seem to have been erased from the city itself. Paris, like the notebook, becomes a surface where time has inscribed itself, only to become unreadable and estranged.

In *The Black Notebook*, writing functions paradoxically as both a tool for remembrance and a means of forgetfulness. This duality reflects the narrator Jean's estrangement from his own memories, as well as from Paris and the physical notebook he carries. Each of these elements—Paris, the notebook, and the reminiscent self—serves as a sign of the self's disconnection from itself. This theme is crystallized in a moment from the novel when Jean, relying on his notebook, attempts to find a hotel he once visited with Dannie. He reflects:

> I tried to find that hotel. I hadn't recorded its name or address in the black notebook, the way we tend not to write down the most intimate details of our lives, for fear that, once fixed on paper, they'll no longer be ours.[22]

In this passage, Jean's notebook is likened to how Jacques Derrida describes a shopping list—a mundane example showing how writing creates a sense of estrangement from the presence of oneself to itself.[23] Even though addressed to the self, a shopping list implies self-absence. The shopping list exemplifies how language—"tomato," "cottage cheese," etc.—acts as a foreign prosthesis: It is foreign because it has to be repeated and understood by others, yet it is intimate as it conditions the referentiality of the self to itself. It is in this sense that Jean's notes signify his dispossession from his memories, as language wanders and is interpreted as detached from the presence of its uttering subject.

While, for Derrida, writing is at play as *arche-writing*, even without being actual as in a notebook or a diary, Jean's notes materialize its self-estrangement in the form of the journal. If we dare to contemplate Derrida's ontological *différance* in historical terms, it certainly insinuates reproducibility. Just as the aura is lost when art is mechanically reproduced, the self is reproduced in writing. The I who writes a shopping list is not the same I who later reads it, just as Jean is not the same person revisiting his old notes. This idea suggests that the self is never fully present to itself but is always a trace of what it once was, making Jean's notebook an example of how writing perpetually separates us from our own experiences and introduces the reproducible conditions of obsolescence into the territory of selfhood.

Jean's voluntary memory illustrates the entanglement of dès vu with difference and writing. As we have seen, dès vu renders the present obsolete from the outset by immediately actualizing it in time—an effort akin to consuming the present to extract its value. In this sense, dès vu functions as inscription: It materializes memory in writing, much like Jean's attempt to safeguard his memories of Dannie for his future self. Yet the paradox lies in the différance inherent to this inscription. Because writing both materializes and alienates, duplicates and estranges, the memories Jean once sought to preserve now appear indecipherable—if not meaningless—to his future self.

Over time, Jean's inability to retrieve memories in a spontaneous and involuntary manner results in a continuous effort to write and rewrite these memories, leading to constant erasure and overlapping notes. Unlike Proust's narrator, Jean's journey begins with the notebook; his memories have always existed within the confines of writing, within the realm of dès vu, where the most intimate details are "no longer ours."[24] No singular unity can be constructed except through the repetitive act of rewriting what is already written. In this respect, Jean's identity is not the only one being rewritten—Dannie and her friends used to adopt false names, playing with elusive signifiers that obscure the truth rather than reveal it. In the novel, the theme of overwriting intertwines with a manuscript Jean lost during the period he now reminisces about. The current Jean does not regret the loss of this manuscript, as he reflects:

> If it hadn't disappeared, I don't think I'd want to write today. Time is abolished and everything starts anew: once again I'm filling pages, with the same kind of pen and the same hand-writing, consulting the jottings in my old notebook as I did before. It has taken

> me almost an entire lifetime to return to my point of departure.[25]

Three overwritten layers emerge from this description: The black notebook, the lost manuscript, and *The Black Notebook*, the text that the present Jean narrates. In the novel's final pages, the entanglement of all three becomes clear. Jean recalls that after losing the manuscript, Dannie had offered that they would glean from booksellers' bins some old and forgotten novels whose readers were long dead; they would copy them by hand and claim they had written them. Following this memory, Jean writes:

> I recalled the opening sentence of my manuscript. . . . I thought that with the help of my black notebook, I could rewrite and improve those lost pages. So in the end, she was right: it would almost feel as if I were copying them. By hand. That's what I'm doing today.[26]

Not only is the black notebook a rewriting of the lost manuscript and *The Black Notebook* itself a rewriting of that notebook, but the act of copying—which, in practice, is a form of rewriting in the absence of reliable memory—is likened to copying another book written by a stranger. This illustrates the experience of a continuous chain of dès vu, now infused with new potential: If the self is inherently prone to becoming an "other," can our connection to others not become as intimate as our relation to ourselves? For Modiano, this potential is realized in *Dora Bruder*, a work that delves into memory through ephemeral traces, though it somewhat deviates from his other novels. In this instance, the narrator investigates the history of someone else—Dora Bruder, a Jewish adolescent who vanished during World War II. In narrating this apparent nonfiction work, Modiano endeavors to trace her journey and illuminate her unknown fate by examining archives, exploring streets, and visiting addresses where she once stayed.

Like the rupture between the past and present versions of Jean, Dora Bruder's story also proves difficult to piece together. The narrative begins with an encounter with an old newspaper advertisement seeking information on the missing Dora, who we learn escaped from her boarding school. From this starting point, Modiano uncovers fragments about Dora, her parents, and their fates during the war; he talks to people who knew them and consults police records. Despite these efforts, the information about Dora remains incomplete at best. Large portions of her life remain unaccounted for. In an attempt to "stay in touch" with Dora during these gaps, Modiano even turns to weather reports to fill in the blanks:

> One way not to lose all touch with Dora Bruder over this period would be to report on the changes in the weather. The first snow fell on 4 November 1941. Winter got off to a cold start on 22 December. On 29 December, the temperature dropped still further, and windowpanes were covered with a thin coating of ice. From 13 January onwards, the cold became Siberian. Water froze. This lasted some four weeks. On 12 February, the sun came out briefly, like a tentative annunciation of spring.[27]

The weather reports parody the wish to regain any sound memory. Dora's past is impossible to fully recover. Instead, the gaps are filled with the narrator's own memories. Modiano walks the streets where he imagines Dora walking: "On Sundays, she would certainly have gone to visit her parents, who were still living in the hotel room at 41 Boulevard Ornano. I look at the plan of the métro and try to retrace her route in my mind."[28] The city, in his work, becomes a space where personal memories intertwine with collective ones. For instance, Modiano refers to his own childhood memories of cinemas on Boulevard Ornano, near the address given in the original newspaper notice about Dora Bruder.[29] Ultimately, Bruder's trajectories become entangled with those of his father ("Perhaps it was that I wanted them to have met, she and my father, in that winter of 1942").[30]

Here too, Modiano's recollections are anything but extemporal. They suffer from all the shortcomings caused by an accelerated passage of time and amnesia. In the same way, for Modiano the past, like Dora, escapes individual possession. That's the conclusion of his search for Dora, in the passage that ends the book:

> I shall never know how she spent her days, where she hid, in whose company she passed the winter months of her first escape, or the few weeks of spring when she escaped for the second time. That is her secret. A poor and precious secret that not even the executioners, the decrees, the occupying authorities, the Dépôt, the barracks, the camps, History, time—everything that defiles and destroys you—have been able to take away from her.[31]

What compensates for her absence, however, is what gives the work its significance: the intertwining of her traces with the personal and the familial, transforming Paris into a stage for the impersonalization of memory. This is impersonal rather than collective memory because each subject's autonomy in the plot is fractured by amnesia, constantly needing an "other"—writing, in Derrida's terms—to make it whole. The immediate estrangement from one's past, the persistent untimeliness of the reminiscent self we associated with Jean, creates an ethical threshold at which the inability to see oneself as anything but a stranger intersects with the ability to be intimately enmeshed in another's memory.

While *Dora Bruder* may not serve as a direct example of dès vu, it helps illuminate how the perception of present experiences as already obsolete facilitates a remembrance characterized by dispossession rather than possession. Jean's dès vu memories could never be fully possessed because they were created as possessions. Capturing the present as memory renders it obsolete and alienated, much like an immediately consumed commodity. Yet this very movement, which prevents the possession of memory by a unified Proustian self, renders our memories as intimate as those of others.

Debt Relief

Susan Rubin Suleiman reads *Dora Bruder* along Paul Ricœur's notion of oneself as another ("Soi même comme un autre"), showing how Modiano enmeshes the autobiographical with the fate of another, casting not only a shadow of himself in Dora Bruder but also of the many other children who suffered her fate.[32] At this point, I want to adopt a similar lens, drawing on Ricœur to discuss the potential that lies in the dispossession produced by the dès vu. I turn to Paul Ricœur's notion of selfhood as narrative identity, which perceives selfhood as something that changes while nevertheless being preserved over time. In the context of dès vu, I will focus on the uncanny counterpart to Ricœur's concept of selfhood—a selfhood rendered obsolete by rejecting its continuity. This selfhood both affirms and negates its past promises and hopes, reflecting a complex interplay between permanence and dispossession. If Derrida focuses on otherness inherent to the self, highlighting the belatedness of any self-presence, Ricœur is interested in how we continually negotiate and redefine the interplay of selfhood and change over time. In *Oneself as Another*, Ricœur distinguishes between two poles of identity: *idem* identity, referring to the unchanging notion of identity such as numerical entities (identity as "sameness"), and *ipse* identity, concerned with selfhood that can persist despite change.[33] For Ricœur, selfhood cannot be reduced to one pole alone, and it is the *ipse* identity pole that is particularly relevant to our exploration of the obsolete.

In dès vu, obsolescence emerges from the interplay of selfhood and time, as memory is no longer mine but becomes that of another. In Ricœur, however, the preservation of selfhood over time, even though it undergoes change, is not something to lament. Rather, literature—particularly narrative—is the space where characters are defined by the changes they undergo (the plot) while remaining recognizable as a singularity. This is why Ricœur refers to *ipse* identity as "narrative identity," because in fiction, "at one end, the character in the story has a definite character, which is identifiable and reidentifiable as the same."[34] The prime example of narrative identity is keeping one's word. Promising encapsulates the paradox of selfhood's preservation over time: In making a promise, we recognize that we change (otherwise, a promise wouldn't be necessary), yet we affirm our selfhood by keeping the promise made in the past. Ricœur writes:

> Self-constancy is for each person that manner of conducting himself or herself so that others can count on that person. Because someone is counting on me, I am accountable for my actions before another. The term "responsibility" unites both meanings: "counting on" and "being accountable for." It unites them, adding the idea of a response to the question "Where are you?" asked by another who needs me. This

> response is the following: "Here I am!" a response that is a statement of self-constancy.[35]

Self-constancy thus becomes an ethical act. The declaration "Here I am" signifies taking responsibility for one's "others," the obsolescent selves, while affirming the continuity of selfhood that persists through time. In this respect, narrative identity acknowledges a self that is constantly actualized yet perpetually obsolete. Its ethical affirmation lies in embracing this endless cycle of transient presences, recognizing that selfhood is defined not by permanence but by its ability to endure through change and loss. In dès vu, however, Ricœur's ethical declaration is inversed. The example I wish to delve into is *The Mortified Podcast*, active since 2015, in which alternating guests read to strangers their diaries, love letters, and chat messages from their teenage years. The podcast, often recorded live at events scattered around the United States, has also been produced as a television format for Netflix as *The Mortified Guide*.

All *Mortified* participants have betrayed their past selves. They read their secret diaries in public, unveiled their most secret wishes, and confided in strangers with details about their high school crushes. The future selves, the evident addressees of these diaries, have preferred to fulfill a present wish rather than a past one. *The Mortified Podcast* is not apologetic about laughing at the dès vu wishes of their teenage versions, who wanted so desperately to try to make their future selves proud with the memorialization of their awkward past experiences. In the first episode on Netflix, "The *Mortified* Guide to Love & Sex," Mandy reads to the audience a fictional sex scene she wrote under the effect of intensifying teenage hormones and Jon Bon Jovi's newly launched *Slippery When Wet*.[36] In the story, she encounters Jon Bon Jovi by chance, and they have sex in the school hall after he offers to help with her stuck locker. In the second episode, Jill reads excerpts from her teenage diary, which she addresses as "Grandpa," mourning for her beloved and deceased grandfather.[37] The mortifying part is that the experiences she confides to her grandpa-diary are not of the kind one would usually share with one's family. In one of the entries she writes: "Dear Grandpa, Jay picked me up two weeks ago and he took me back to his 'apartment.' We hooked up."[38]

With Modiano, we have seen how the personal diary, as a very voluntary form of inscribing memories, renders memories inevitably untimely in already anticipating the future reader, a reader who is always estranged from the now belated memory. All the while, memories are written exactly to be remembered in the future and thus preserved. This paradoxical logic involves the preservation of memories only at the expense of dispossessing them. Only this dispossession can allow the peculiar doubling that happens on the *Mortified* stage: The grown-up self reads their diary as the one who is intimately associated with it, while another part of them can laugh ironically, as do the spectators in the audience, as if the memories and mortifying diary entries were entirely someone else's. The fact that we all have been teenagers and can understand what they are like allows a new form of impersonality to emerge: We laugh at a story of an individual but also at all the capricious teenagers in the world, including the teenagers we once were.

The *Mortified* participants come to terms with their past selves publicly, enacting this betrayal but also relieving a debt. This is the double sense of dès vu, which makes it much more than a lamentation for the loss of a present moment to become a memory. In the grown-up world, perhaps regrettably, it is better to become disenchanted from an unrelenting sexual fixation on Jon Bon Jovi. Calculating the "grand total" of one's sexual acts, as the teenage Misha had done in the first episode of "The *Mortified* Guide," exemplifies a similar futile attempt to secure the capital of the present for the future. This effort is ultimately doomed to fail: The adult Misha neither accepts nor rejects the credit and debt imposed upon her by her past self. Instead, in sharing her story with a crowd of strangers—where impersonality is embedded in the experience—she is dispossessed of that debt, which is, in fact, not uniquely hers but shared by many others.

"The *Mortified* Guide" shows how the initial duplication of the self in the memory of the present is an essential but also acceptable element in the establishment of the self, which is always in the process of becoming-obsolete. The ability to eschew so harshly the wishes of the past is the liberating fulfillment of the potential within this duplication and doubling: discovering a new intimacy with oneself and others, through the view of oneself as another. If dès vu is perceived as a word given for a future self, one aligned with the logic of a promise, it becomes evident that the participants in *The Mortified Podcast* do not keep their word. The promise made to their future selves, in the form of dès vu memories inscribed in diaries, is dismissed, as though they are saying the inverse of Ricœur's declaration: "Here is *no longer* 'I am.'" Through the force of this inversion, they fulfill Ricœur's thinking to its fullest extent, by conceiving oneself as another and thus the other as the self.

Dancing with Past Selves

My aim is neither to offer additional commentary on Derridean différance nor to provide an in-depth analysis of Ricœur's interpretation of memory in narrative. Rather, this trajectory is essential for understanding the interplay between consumption and obsolescence—not only in the realm of commodities but within the economy of memory and selfhood, which is precisely the way dès vu operates. The fact that writing inscribes a "no longer" form of the present brings Derrida's thought into the realm of obsolescence, as dès vu actualizes the present in a similar manner when framing it for future use. The inevitable alienation of the future self from the past self, a central concern in Derridean thought, takes on a mnemonic-economic dimension in dès vu: The present is not only inscribed but framed as a discarded commodity.

With Ricœur, this trajectory expands from the moment of inscription to the framework of narrative identity. Here, the obsolete self—holding an obsolete currency—cannot be seamlessly integrated into a coherent self-narration. The cringing hopes and desires of the past fracture self-narration to the point that liberation is found not in reaffirming personal identity but in its inversion—transforming memory into something impersonal. In this sense, reclaiming the disposal of past promises within a shared realm, rather than within a self-calculated economy of memory, becomes an act of release.

The necessary step forward is to move from the economy of selfhood back to the economy of obsolete objects and media to clarify their entanglement. The inherent outdatedness of selfhood, as explored thus far, prefigures a contemporary drama in which technological obsolescence becomes pervasive. Obsolete media, preserving fragments of past selves—their hopes, promises, and awkward or embarrassing moments—anchors the experience of viewing oneself as another. These discarded pasts, embedded in obsolete formats, echo motifs from horror films, where neglected technologies (such as the VHS tapes in *The Ring*) serve as conduits for ghostly or unresolved presences. The ontological form of obsolescence is thus central to understanding these emerging digital specters, introducing a materialization of Derrida's shopping list logic yet grounding it in specific historical conditions.

A compelling case study is the theatrical performance *Greetings from the Past*, in which obsolete media accentuates the unsettling distance between past and present selves through the awkwardness and dissonance of self-confrontation.[39] Directed by Renana Raz and Nitzan Cohen and based on Klaudia Hartung-Wójciak's project *User's Manual for Your Past Which I've Never Seen*, the performance invites participants to revisit moments from their past, retrieved from old VHS tapes, while narrating and negotiating their new meanings. The VHS tapes—an obsolete medium no longer integrated into contemporary life—function as more than mere metaphor. In their analog fragility, prone to cracking, slowing, and degradation, they disrupt the ways we decode their content. This material resistance mirrors the difficulty of assimilating dès vu memories: Just as the obsolete medium obstructs smooth playback, past selves resist incorporation into the present.

One participant, Corinne Kitzis, confronts a series of dès vu moments from her early twenties, recorded with her video camera—waxing her legs, crying after a breakup, confiding in the camera before falling asleep. She follows one of Hartung-Wójciak's imperatives from the manual, which instructs her to write down the names, ages, and details of those who held the camera and then to "shoot them—but not really." The verb *shoot*, with its dual meaning of filming and aiming to kill, imbues the encounter with charged ambivalence. On stage, Kitzis faces her younger self—an insecure woman who compulsively films herself with her portable Sony camera out of fear of being alone (fig. 3). The camera is not merely a memory aid; it is a companion.

In the present, Kitzis begins to mimic the gestures of her filmed past self: sobbing in sync with her twenty-year-old self on screen, then dancing alongside her to Tony Holiday's "Tanze Samba mit mir" ("Dance the Samba with Me"). In this act of repetition, she attempts to recapture her younger self, to close the gap and affirm their continuity.

Yet paradoxically, the more she tries to mirror the past, the more she exposes the distance that time has created between them. The difference is not fully articulable, but it is felt in the act of repetition. Even though the movements are the same, they are not, because time has irreversibly altered their meaning. Kitzis attempts to read her past self, but the dance becomes clumsy. Eventually, the younger Kitzis exits the video frame, and the present Kitzis continues dancing alone. Her liberation lies not in proving continuity with her past self but in acknowledging their unbridgeable difference—what begins as reenactment becomes, instead, a performance of estrangement, a recognition that time has turned her into someone else.

Figure 3. Corinne Kitzis in *Greetings from the Past*. Photo by Aviv Nave.

The analog VHS produces diachronic difference rather than synchronic continuation. Just as an obsolete format like the VHS tape cannot simply be read by the already obsolete DVD player, Kitzis cannot fully "play back" or decipher her own past self. She is condemned to misread her past. She is still "her," but in a way that resists seamless legibility: recognizable yet indecipherable, proximate yet opaque. At the same time, the performance shows how the existence of obsolete promises and hopes—whether in digital archives or outdated formats—is not solely a source of shame. If the dès vu bears ethical stakes, indeed, it lies in inhabiting intimate others, in relinquishing the fantasy of a unified, up-to-date self.

Encounters with obsolete hopes, fantasies, and memories emerge from a disposable orientation toward time, one in which the present is consumed and swiftly discarded. But, as we increasingly remember in immediate and synchronic ways, the past grows more indecipherable, and it is through misreading and misappropriation that diachronic time prevails. In the shift from déjà vu to dès vu—from involuntary, auratic memory to its deliberate counterpart—these enigmatic pasts become sites of refuge from the relentless drive toward novelty. Within the temporal cycle of presentism, material and digital archives hold the potential to transform into a collective claim on the past—a past that transcends personal possession precisely because it was so desperately meant to be owned.

2
Nonimages

András István Arató, a retired engineer from Hungary, is better known in internet culture as Hide the Pain Harold, a meme originating from a stock photo of Arató that began circulating online in 2011. After retiring, Arató became a model for stock photography platforms, portraying roles such as a doctor, a carpenter, and, most famously, a man working on his laptop with a strained smile (fig. 4). This particular image became the basis for his internet fame, circulating as a meme on platforms such as 4Chan and symbolizing the archetype of a fake smile meant to conceal inner discomfort ("Hide the Pain"). Since gaining internet notoriety, Arató has reclaimed his fame. He took part in a Coca-Cola video advertisement, shared his story on a TED platform, and started selling merchandise through an official Instagram account.[1]

The photograph that launched the meme, originally taken by the user Nyul and titled "Mature man using computer, drinking tea, looking at camera, smiling," exemplifies the performative logic of contemporary visual culture. In this media ecology, images circulate rapidly across social platforms and advertising spaces, functioning as a grammar for expressing authenticity—while always already contaminated by performativity. As Hito Steyerl argues in her essay on the "poor image," digital low-resolution, degraded visuals—circulated beyond their original contexts—become the "debris of audiovisual production, the trash that washes up on the digital economies' shores."[2] These images, she writes, are "dragged around the globe as commodities or their effigies, as gifts or as bounty."[3]

The stock image, however, introduces a different kind of afterlife. Designed for timeless applicability, it is stripped of any contextual markers that might anchor it to a specific moment. Arató's portrait, in this sense, functions not as a degraded image but as a nonimage: a deliberately generic construction intended to resist obsolescence. Arató embodies an abstract archetype of the older white man at work. His laptop is brandless, the apartment stripped of identifiers, evoking a vaguely European Airbnb-IKEA aesthetic that suits everyone and no one in particular. This erasure of specificity anticipates the photo's use in multiple settings, from retirement blogs to nursing home ads.

If Steyerl locates the subversive potential of the poor image in its democratized degradation, the nonimage derives its unsettling power from its preemptive obsolescence. It resists time by design, yet in doing so becomes temporally uncanny—a form of semiotic residue circulating because it carries a faint semantic charge. Arató's attempt to embody the stock archetype of the "mature man using a computer" situates his photograph within the realm of unintentional camp: a visual form that, in trying too hard to appear authentic, collapses under the weight of its own formatting.

As explored throughout this book, obsolescence is not only a condition of things but increasingly a condition of selves. Photography, and particularly the photographic forms that stage the self for circulation, is a means of tracing how the visual performance of identity internalizes the logic of obsolescence. I focus here on two paradigmatic forms: the dès vu image and the stock image. While dès vu images enact temporal immediacy—designed to be posted, seen, and forgotten—stock photographs aspire to generic timelessness, rendering them paradoxically obsolete from the outset. Both forms embody a performative aesthetic structured by disposability and repetition, and both reveal the tension between authenticity and performativity in networked selfhood.

The presentist cultural imperative is to exhibit a "true," authentic self, and authenticity appears to promise resistance to obsolescence—it offers a vision of the self as grounded, coherent, and enduring. Yet under conditions of contemporary visual culture and social media, in which selfhood is in a constant acceleration of discarding and reformulating attachments, authenticity is itself formatted, staged, and circulated. As Michelle Gorea argues, in contemporary networked culture, the true self is "re-workable as images are connected through a variety of networked practices."[4] In this context, authenticity becomes subject to the very forces it seeks to escape: Once performed for cyclic consumption, the desire to appear authentic becomes a source of cringe and retrospective scrutiny.

Stock photography becomes a particularly revealing case study, mirroring presentism in its aspiration toward endless recyclability. Designed for repetitive application, it disavows specificity in order to maximize circulation. Yet what aspires to be timeless instead becomes drained of content: a visual shell that cannot act as an effective commodity. As I show later in the chapter, this logic is pushed to its limits in the register of performative identity and camp, where the image's attempt to signify authenticity collapses into affective excess and aesthetic cliché. Camp, in this sense, does not resist obsolescence—it exaggerates it, exposing the theatricality at the heart of any visual selfhood.

Figure 4: The original stock photograph of Hide the Pain Harold. Photo by Nyul (Dreamstime).

The Generic Image

The origins of stock photography as an independent industry can be traced back to the 1970s, marked by a relative standardization of its modus operandi. Within this system, stock photography agencies maintain "stocks" of images taken by freelance photographers, which they sell to clients in the marketing and journalistic sectors.[5] In the 1990s, the introduction of the "royalty-free" category allowed clients to purchase the rights to use an image as many times as desired.[6] This evolution fostered the creation of generic, timeproof images designed for recycling across multiple contexts.

A significant milestone came with the integration of the industry into the World Wide Web, giving rise to highly popular stock databases like Shutterstock and Getty Images. These platforms utilize user information to predict and monitor the success of their inventory while offering large portions of their stock for free download. As Paul Frosh explains,

"In an age in which images have become both abundant and unprecedentedly accessible, the commercial-industrial production of photography begins what may be part of an epochal shift from the mass manufacture of pictures to the mass processing of viewers."[7] Today, the industry has been integrated into the generative AI revolution, largely continuing under the same generic aesthetics of the pre-AI stock photo.

Frosh defines the generic image associated with stock photography as both referentially and interpretively ambivalent.[8] It is referentially ambivalent because it is staged and therefore indexicality rooted in an unreal occurrence. It is interpretively ambivalent because it is polysemic, created to be used repeatedly in diverse contexts. These two features of the generic image are critical to understanding its performativity. While purportedly enacting an ordinary moment ("mature man drinking tea"), its generic staging produces an impression of ordinariness vague enough to transcend the effects of time. Stock photography does not "capture a moment"; instead, its mission is to endure beyond any particular instance, beyond time itself.

In the visual culture of presentism, the stock photo exemplifies a tendency toward transformable recycling rather than straightforward reuse. For this reason, a stock photograph, as suggested by guides for stock photographers, should feature a clean background clear of distractions.[9] It should avoid identifiable elements, such as visible brand names or graffiti-scarred park benches in the background. The image should be harmonious and exclude anything associated with cigarettes, alcohol, clutter, fads, miserable elderly people, depressing locations, or fast food.[10] Stock photography reproduces—and simultaneously constructs—the soothing ambience often tied to consumption: an ex-temporal space devoid of conflict. If the nonplace is the spatial paradigm of postindustrial consumption, the stock photo is its visual counterpart: a "nonimage."

The potential for recycling across multiple contexts is, in

fact, the primary consideration in the generic manufacturing of the stock image—its very raison d'être. Consider Ariane, a Canadian-Chinese stock photography model and the focus of the Facebook group "Ariane—the Overexposed Stock Image Model."[11] Ariane's portraits appear globally in various contexts: as a backpacker, an accountant, a saleswoman, or a tourist with her partner. The same smiling photo might simultaneously promote e-SIM services, travel insurance, and laser hair removal.

The conditions that make Ariane suitable for such diverse products are multifaceted. The evolution of the online stock photography industry has made it easier than ever to purchase and use royalty-free images that can be endlessly repurposed for advertisements, magazines, and brand websites. The style of photographs featuring Ariane, characteristic of generic stock imagery, is intentionally clear, conflict-free, and decontextualized—a visual commodity designed to be endlessly adaptable to a variety of clients' needs. Equally significant is Ariane herself. Her appearance carries a universal appeal: relatable, inclusive, and with an ethnicity not easily categorized in a single context, making her photos especially popular among global advertisers. In stock photography, Ariane embodies a familiar version of the young, aspirational woman—traveling the world with her partner, pursuing a promising career, or selecting the best travel insurance.

To achieve this endless recyclability, Ariane's portraits must remain semiotically impoverished, meticulously avoiding any *punctum*—that is, any detail that might disrupt their seamless adaptability. Yet in defying its own obsolescence, the nonimage also challenges the photographic medium itself, as it was conceived in the canonical theory of photography. Susan Sontag famously described photography as an inventory of mortality.[12] For Sontag, by capturing a transient fragment of time, photography instills a posthumous irony, reflecting on the inevitable passage of time and its transformative force.[13] The referentially ambivalent generic photo replaces this irony with a contradictory sensation. In its ultimate form, the generic photo's referent is general enough to transcend temporality. The act of capturing is not a lamentation of a past moment, as no such moment ever occurred. Instead, it creates a specter-photograph—neither dead nor alive.

In the same vein, the generic stock photo denies the photograph its "here it is" effect, as theorized by Roland Barthes. For Barthes, the "here it is" effect is tied to the indexical value of photography: The photo represents something specific and "real," as "a specific photograph, in effect, is never distinguished from its referent."[14] This essential effect is absent in a generic, staged photograph, where the referents are defined by their lack of particularity. In aspiring to ex-temporality, the generic photo becomes a radicalized version of a fully *studium* photograph. While the studium, according to Barthes, is the cultural framework of an image, the punctum is an "accident that pricks"—something particular within the image that draws the viewer's attention and provokes an affective response. Barthes, for example, characterizes news photographs as having no punctum. These images provide "a certain shock—the literal can traumatize—but no disturbance; the photograph can 'shout,' not wound."[15] In other words, news photographs aim to shock but remain confined to predefined meanings, lacking anything singular or personal to provoke the viewer.

Barthes's punctum is inseparable from an anchoring of the image in time. Toward the end of *Camera Lucida*, Barthes defines time itself as punctum. Addressing Alexander Gardner's photograph of Lewis Payne just before his execution, Barthes writes:

> The photograph is handsome, as is the boy; that is the *studium*. But the *punctum* is: he is going to die. I read at the same time: *This will be* and *This has been*; I

> observe with horror an anterior future of which death is at stake. By giving me the absolute past of the pose (aorist), the photograph tells me death in the future.[16]

Barthes's example is rhetorically intricate, its reasoning excessive. Payne's literal execution supplements the argument that every photograph is, in a sense, an execution. Time, as punctum, lies in the photograph's freezing of a moment within the overarching context of mortality. Every photograph points to something that will inevitably die. Here, the generic stock photo stands as an absolute outsider. Staged and abstract, referentially weak and designed to be time-proof, the stock photo is crafted to evade this punctum by remaining a studium for as long as possible.

Disposable Moments

Unlike the generic nonimage, the dès vu, in its form as an image, does not reject this photographic essence; instead, it accelerates its central traits. Photography, as a medium that captures the present, inherently carries a melancholic relationship with the outdated—it strives to arrest time, yet it is enmeshed with the mourning of its "already pastness." For Benjamin, photography disrupts the aura of involuntary memory, democratizing memory while anchoring it in reproducible form: "If the distinctive feature of the images that rise from the *mémoire involontaire* is seen in their aura, then photography is decisively implicated in the phenomenon of the 'decline of the aura.'"[17] In this light, dès vu is inseparable from the democratization of photography in modernity. With cloud archiving promising to save everything, the future becomes preemptively past; the smartphone camera renders every moment accessible as memory, preserving the present for later consumption.

Consider Andrew D. Bernstein's iconic photograph of

LeBron James breaking Kareem Abdul-Jabbar's NBA scoring record. Bernstein's image not only captures LeBron's shot in mid-air but also the crowd's collective act of filming the moment with their smartphones—a visual manifestation of dès vu. Here, the use of smartphones allows fans to experience the event as already a memory, framing it through their own devices. The photo quickly became emblematic of digital-age criticism, lamenting an inability to "be in the moment." Yet Bernstein's image complicates these critiques. While it is tempting to praise the few spectators who did not use their phones, dès vu is already an internalized mode of experience. The smartphones themselves are merely an extension of a deeper cultural lens through which the present is apprehended as memory. Photography, long before smartphones and social media, has commodified the present. In order to commodify a present we need to make an object out of it, and this is exactly, as Sontag argues, what the camera does:

> To photograph people is to violate them, by seeing them as they never see themselves, by having knowledge of them they can never have; it turns people into objects that can be symbolically possessed. Just as the camera is a sublimation of the gun, to photograph someone is a sublimated murder—a soft murder, appropriate to a sad, frightened time.[18]

For Sontag, all photographs function as memento mori, participating in the mortality and mutability of their objects:

> To take a photograph is to participate in another person's (or thing's) mortality, vulnerability, mutability. Precisely by slicing out this moment and freezing it, all photographs testify to time's relentless melt.[19]

In Sontag's critique, photography is intertwined with outdatedness. Freezing the present is an act of pinning it in time, and from that moment forward, it becomes an unreachable past. The dès vu mechanism, as its photographic application, actualizes the present and transforms it into memory, rendering it irretrievable. Bernstein's photograph demonstrates that dès vu is deeply embedded in photography's engagement with time, predating digital media. However, the proliferation of smartphones in the image foregrounds the connection between dès vu and the visual culture of presentism. Everyone in the Crypto.com Arena knew the historic moment was being documented by professionals, televised live, and widely shared. Yet each individual sought to capture the moment for personal possession—whether for social media or to store in a smartphone gallery, destined to join countless other forgotten images.

Barthes, meanwhile, connects photography with self-awareness and self-mourning, elucidating the performative dimensions of the dès vu image rather than its mere indexicality. In *Camera Lucida*, he reflects on the process of objectification when facing a camera:

> But very often (too often, to my taste) I have been photographed and knew it. Now, once I feel myself observed by the lens, everything changes: I constitute myself in the process of "posing," I instantaneously make another body for myself, I transform myself in advance into an image.[20]

The present moment, aware of its transformation into memory, becomes a self-conscious and staged event. Barthes describes this as a microversion of death: "I am truly becoming a specter."[21] This performative act completes the dès vu experience, as the dès vu photograph represents a duplication of the self and an awareness of one's own mortality. By this, Barthes shows how the dès vu entails an internalization of the photographic medium into selfhood—positioning the self performatively, as something to be seen and addressed. Yet, as emphasized in the previous chapter, the very act of actualization—which Sontag so poignantly connects to the photographic act—transforms this performative condition into one of consumption. I do not merely internalize the imperative to be seen; I also come to understand myself as an image in circulation, governed by a logic of actualization, exhaustion, and obsolescence.

The photographic entanglement with dès vu positions it in direct contrast to the nonimage. Bernstein's LeBron James photo is a memory from its inception, while the generic stock photo remains amnesiac. Photography's intrinsic link to mortality—exemplified by dès vu's reflective gaze—stands in opposition to the nonimage's aspiration to timelessness. Yet both dès vu images and nonimages are products of a fixation on presentism. Each commodifies the present: one through ephemeral disposability, the other through timeless applicability. Together, they expose a performative mechanism that stages the present as endlessly consumable yet perpetually out of reach, raising crucial questions about the stakes of this performative tendency—questions I will now explore through the specific form of the selfie.

See Me (Showing You Myself)

Every photograph of us signifies our death, imbued with a dual awareness: We recognize our own process of becoming-object and the present as inevitably becoming obsolete. While this dès vu feeling has been embedded in photography since its inception, it is radicalized in the age of smartphones, where the photographer and the photographed are often identical—capturing themselves in a selfie. Exploiting the ephemeral capturing of photography, the selfie transforms the photograph into a fleeting personal performance, one destined to languish among digital debris.

The selfie, as Frosh suggests, manipulates the traditional

indexical nature of the photograph. According to Frosh, "the selfie as an index is less the trace of a reality imprinted on the photograph than of an action enacted by a photographer," while, in addition, "the selfie exploits indexicality in favor of connective performance rather than semantic reference."[22] The selfie is performative in the sense that the reality imprinted in the photograph is inferior to the simple fact that the photograph was taken and, by proxy, that a particular being was in a particular place at a particular time. The deixis of the photograph, the brute fact that it points to something that took place, was knowingly proclaimed by Barthes as the *noeme* of photography in *Camera Lucida*: the "here it is!" quality of every photograph.[23] With the selfie, however, the gesture of mediation is radicalized, as the producer and the referent are the same: "It says not only 'see this, here, now,' but 'see me showing you me.'"[24]

This logic is associated with smartphone-produced snapshots even beyond the selfie. In the LeBron James photograph, seemingly the referent was LeBron James. But we have seen how light the referential weight of James is for each one of the snapshots, considering the fact that the moment was broadcast on TV and captured by professional photographers. Rather, the referent of each one of the hundreds of snapshots taken in the crowd was the producers themselves—when there is no need for the "see this, here, now" dimension of the photograph, what is left is "see me showing you me (seeing this, here, now)."

The performative value of the selfie, rather than its indexicality, is what renders it, in the words of the contemporary author Maria Stepanova, "trash" that "keeps piling up forever."[25] Whereas the traditional portrait aspires to capture the essence of its referent, the selfie records only its dissolution and eventual disappearance. Stepanova articulates this paradox: "What photography now registers is nothing other than the body of death: the part of me that has no personal will or choice, which anyone can claim, which is fixed and preserved without effort. It is the part that dies, and not the part that remains."[26] In an intriguing reversal, she frames the selfie—intended as a means of preservation—as a mere residue, an accumulation of detritus, while the true essence of the self ultimately eludes the impulse to capture it.

Stepanova's *In Memory of Memory*, an eclectic work on remembrance combining the memoir, the essay, and some other genres of writing, dedicates a compelling chapter to photography in the contemporary moment, suggesting an alternative to the performativity of the selfie. The chapter, "Sex and the Dead," begins with a found photograph capturing a naked woman, a photograph that certainly was not meant to be found: "I'd turned up at the wrong time, and in the wrong place, and I'd witnessed what I shouldn't have witnessed: sex," writes Stepanova.[27] The sex photograph was left orphaned. Unlike a dès vu, it does not claim anything beyond its doing. It captures a moment shared by two people meant for nobody to interrupt: "We know only two things about these people: that they are dead and that they had no interest in bequeathing their bodies to eternity."[28]

In what sense does the selfie, which like dès vu not only captures a moment but creates it as a memory, produce a memory already dead? Barthes already implies this in *Camera Lucida*, claiming that photography is never, in essence, a memory, but a "counter-memory."[29] The photograph is only a quotation of a memory, as it lacks the depth, odor, or music a memory has. A true memory is aligned with the Bergsonian *durée*, an experienced time indivisible into units and spatial measurements. Memory is vivid; a photograph is static. For Stepanova, then, digital photography radicalizes the temptation to quote and arrest time—and this is why the piles of photographs that aim at remembering actually signifying amnesia and oblivion. The past is gone, and we are left with its waste and residues.

Both Barthes and Stepanova embrace the terminology of death and waste to elaborate on this point. In a foresight, Barthes addresses the young photographers who aim at capturing actuality but are, in fact, "agents of Death."[30] In the same way the dès vu actualizes the becoming-past of the present, that is, its obsolescence—photography stands for an actualization that blocks the possibility of memory. This terminology of death, a "flat death" in Barthes's terms, is therefore mixed up with obsolescence when he claims that

> the only way I can transform the Photograph is into refuse: either the drawer or the wastebasket. Not only does it commonly have the fate of paper (perishable), but even if it is attached to more lasting supports, it is still mortal: like a living organism, it is born on the level of the sprouting silver grains, it flourishes a moment, then ages.[31]

Using similar terminology, Stepanova shows how the obsolescence of the actual photograph does not disappear with the digital age. This is because the old photograph does not only age, die, or disappear. To the contrary, the dead photograph lingers. It is not "dead" when it is compared to waste and junk—but simply obsolete is the destiny that was given to it, as we have seen, by the very conditions of its creation.

Stepanova's discussion of the selfie emphasizes that the true antidote to the selfie must avoid performativity. If the desire to perform the present renders a photograph disposable, accumulating as digital debris, then the only photograph that could resonate with the melancholia of Barthes and Sontag—the nonaccelerated form of an obsolete present—must be indifferent to its future spectators. Stepanova reenacts the Bergsonian logic of mnemonic utility, with triumphing indecipherable memories set against excessively voluntary memories so readily captured for immediate use. Again, it is a distinction between the involuntary and the voluntary, between the déjà vu and the dès vu, which is at the core of the discussion. In the compelling paragraphs concluding Stepanova's chapter on photography, it is the former that opens a path to meaningful relations with our past:

> Maybe that's why I love photographs that need no interlocutor and have no desire to engage with me. They are, in their own way, rehearsals for nonexistence, for life without us, for the time when the room is no longer ours to enter. A family is drinking tea, the children are playing chess; the general bends over the map; the baker's assistant lays out the cakes—and we can satisfy our ancient and enduring desire to gaze into every one of the windows of the house of a thousand windows.[32]

Just like the found photograph of a naked woman, Stepanova is fascinated by all of those antiselfies, photographs indifferent to their future viewers. If the selfie, as we have seen, following Frosh, is not a lot more than proof of existence, photographs with "no interlocutors" are a glimpse into nonexistence. These are the photos of our ancestors that were not designated for the family album, left on the cutting room floor:

> Photographs which failed to live up to the photographer's hopes are the unrealized scraps from a manufacturing process: a running dog, blurred to an unending streak, someone's shoes on a wet pavement, a chance passer-by in the frame. All this waste was filtered out and destroyed in the age of printing on paper. But now these very pictures have a special attraction because they were not intended for us (or for anyone). They

> belong to no one and so they belong to me—these moments which survived by accident and are freed from all obligation, stolen from life by life itself. These images of people are utterly impersonal and this is their advantage: they relieve the viewer of the burden of succession, historical memory, bad conscience, and a sense of indebtedness towards the dead.[33]

The filtered past may not offer an ex-temporal unity, but it can certainly offer a break from an unremitting economy of debt, mastery, and possession. Photographs that do not fixate on preservation are freed from the cumbersome need to preserve and possess the present. They allow us, even momentarily, to be free of debt, whether a debt to other people or, in the case of dès vu, a debt we imposed upon ourselves. In allowing the photograph to linger in its obsolescence outside a cultural cycle of debt and recycling, both we and the referents (which are most of the time ourselves) can take a nonartificial breath of relief.

Performative Presents

Rather than a rehearsal for nonexistence, the stock photograph is created with the appropriation of its future spectators in mind. Stepanova's appreciation of indifferent photographs is significant here, as her critique targets photographs that fail to perform their own exhaustion—images created under conditions that desperately anticipate their addressees. In this respect, the generic image mirrors the selfie-taker by enacting its future interpretation: Models posing as a cheerful group of coworkers, for example, embody the image's exhaustive use in business contexts, much like the selfie-taker enacts the sentiment of "Here I am, showing you this." Like the selfie, it wants to be appropriated, and it wants it too much.

In our discussion of the dès vu, we examined how misreading—a time capsule received in unintended ways—charges encounters with the obsolete with the weight of duration. However, as I suggested at the outset of this chapter, our focus now shifts to the ways in which the nonimage invites misappropriation, particularly because of its performative aesthetics. The nonimage, designed for future consumption, operates through the most conventional interpretations of cultural signs. The stock photographer must decide what a "man working on his laptop" looks like, just as they must determine how a business meeting should appear or how to depict abstract emotions such as happiness or anger. In this way, generic images function as a cultural encoder and decoder, one aiming to imitate—and therefore interpret and define—the most mundane aspects of everyday culture.

What stock photography thus exposes is the *realness* of the ordinary. In queer ballroom culture, realness involves mimicking hegemonic and heteronormative appearances to the point of transparency, aiming to pass seamlessly without inviting scrutiny. For instance, "femme queen realness" refers to passing as a cisgender woman outside the ballroom. Judith Butler, in her analysis of the 1990 film *Paris Is Burning*, highlights the subversive nature of realness within ballroom culture, where "the contest (which we might read as a 'contesting of realness') involves the phantasmatic attempt to approximate realness, but it also exposes the norms that regulate realness as themselves phantasmatically instituted and sustained."[34] This reflects Butler's broader theorization of drag and performative gender: Realness both mimics and deconstructs, fantasizes and disrupts.

By mastering the semiotics of hegemonic norms, ballroom participants expose their contingency. The performativity of the nonimage mirrors this dynamic, extending realness beyond gender roles to encompass neoliberal norms. What is ultimately revealed is the artifice of phantasmatically instituted ordinariness. What constitutes "woman-walking-on-the-street realness"? "Kids-playing realness"? "Terrorist-attack realness"? Stock photography, with its vast repository of visual imaginaries, becomes a kind of ballroom where ordinariness itself is in drag.

Realness becomes recognizable as a form only by distinguishing itself from the merely "real." In *Paris Is Burning*, Butler notes that the "double movement of approximating and exposing the phantasmatic status of the realness norm" is reinforced by the juxtaposition of scenes showing "real" people in expensive stores against ballroom performances.[35] This differentiation highlights the tension between neutral, transparent "realness" (e.g., passersby on the street) and the ballroom version of realness, which exposes the constructed nature of the first. Ballroom realness aspires to perfect imitation but never fully achieves it, whether because of context (emerging from the ballroom rather than the streets) or form (imitating the "real" without completely becoming it). In some places, passing as "real" can be perilous; the tragic fate of Venus Xtravaganza, as depicted in *Paris Is Burning*, who was murdered after passing as a cisgender woman, underscores this danger.[36]

In this respect, the success of realness paradoxically entails its failure. This paradox is embedded in the aesthetics of the nonimage, whose distinct visual language is instantly recognizable—an effect exemplified by the 2015 promotional campaign for *Unfinished Business*.[37] The film's cast was photographed mimicking business stock photos: clean backgrounds, forced smiles, and formulaic office interactions. By parodying the genre, the campaign underscored its central contradiction—its attempt at transparency is never fully realized. Because the generic image is spectral, resisting attachment to a specific moment or context, it aims for universal applicability. Yet this very quality prevents stock photos from passing as authentic; instead, they produce a drag effect—an exaggeration of banality.

Like camp style, stock photography heightens clichés, such as the archetypal mature man smiling with a cup of tea. Its exaggerated performance invites reinterpretation and critique, as evidenced by the viral humor surrounding Hide the Pain Harold. Camp, as Sontag argued, foregrounds identities within quotation marks: "It's not a lamp, but a 'lamp'; not a woman, but a 'woman.'"[38] The essence of camp lies in failed seriousness—earnest attempts to convey meaning that inadvertently become humorous or absurd. Nothing is campier than a serious effort to communicate a definitive cultural meaning: "The Art Nouveau craftsman who makes a lamp with a snake coiled around it is not kidding, nor is he trying to be charming. He is saying, in all earnestness: Voila! the Orient!"[39] In a very similar way, stock photography proclaims, "Voila! A mature man drinking tea," while its sincere attempt to capture a cultural identity is exposed as an asymptotic performance—that is, as camp.

Stock photography's claim to "realness" lies in its aspiration to transcend time. But camp, rather than mourning obsolescence, finds creativity in discarded trends. Sontag points out the affinity of camp for old-fashioned objects, suggesting that the process of aging provides the necessary detachment to approach them with sympathy: What once appeared banal can, over time, become "fantastic."[40] Andrew Ross pushes this point further:

> This knowledge about history is the precise moment when camp takes over, because camp is a rediscovery of history's waste. Camp irreverently retrieves not only that which had been excluded from the serious high-cultural "tradition," but also the more unsalvageable material that has been picked over and found wanting by purveyors of the "antique." For the

> camp liberator, as with the high modernist, history's waste matter becomes all too available as a "ragbag," but irradiated, this time around, with glamor, and not drenched with tawdriness by the mock-heroism of Waste Land irony. But, in "liberating" the past in this way, it also bolsters the economy whereby objects and discourses of disdain are transformed into collector's items. Camp, in this respect, is more than just a remembrance of things past; it is *the re-creation of surplus value from forgotten forms of labor.*[41]

As a celebration of bad taste, camp fixates on the obsolete nature of its style. Camp does not employ fashionable antiques but rather shocking, obsolete forms—specifically those that the present cannot assimilate, not even as rebranded retro chic. Camp's appropriation is eerie not because it transcends representation fixed at a specific point in time but because it deliberately emphasizes this timestamp to the point of excessive, ironic exaggeration. By redeeming stamped styles while foregrounding the affective charge of their very outdatedness, camp's irony demonstrates a sensitivity to history and a disenchantment with pop culture's relentless craving for the timely.

The same tendency of the generic image to perform for future consumption is turned against itself, as its desire for "realness" could be stamped in time by means of decoding and interpretation. Hide the Pain Harold attempts to embody "mature-man-drinking-tea" realness, and through this earnest effort to project an identity, it opens itself up to subversive reinterpretations. These reinterpretations are illustrated by the transformation of Hide the Pain Harold into a disposable meme, repurposed repeatedly in varying contexts to deliver different "Hide the Pain" messages. Examples include captions such as "When it's April 2nd, and your life's still a joke" or "Someone stole my identity—hope they make something out of my life." One of the most popular interpretations of Hide the Pain Harold reimagines this stock-photo character through a humorous narrative presented in a YouTube video by ChinnyxD.[42] The video alternates between various stock photos featuring András István Arató: playing cards with his wife ("she just can't stop cheating"), drinking wine ("better drink away your problems"), using a calculator ("Harold is a responsible taxpayer"), and more.

This playful reinterpretation resonates to a surprising degree with queer practices of reading, which aim to negotiate performative identities—such as the realness of "being a responsible citizen"—and, in doing so, expose the contingency of what constitutes citizenship responsibility. While the stock photograph aspires to bypass obsolescence, its campiness invites scrutiny, undermining its intended neutrality. Through camp and reading, time reintegrates into the generic image: Every supposedly "universal" message that the stock photo seeks to convey is reappropriated, anchored within a specific historical moment and cultural context in which it is *used* rather than being transparently recycled.

Hide the Pain Harold was so intent on being endlessly recyclable that its very lightness—its lack of content and its adaptability—ultimately turned against it. The trajectory of this image epitomizes a visual language of failed authenticity: a mode of representation that aims to convey sincerity while being structurally formatted for circulation and consumption. In a culture that craves "true selves" yet accelerates the transformation of identity into image, Harold's portrait attempts to immunize itself from time by avoiding specificity. But this very effort to escape temporal anchoring reveals its underlying performativity—a metonym for a visual culture in which selfhood is exposed as inherently performative, perpetually transformable, and therefore always at the risk of obsolescence.

3
Old Flames

The fleeting romantic encounter, the one-night stand, encapsulates the tension between instant gratification and inevitable obsolescence. It offers swift infatuation, only to be discarded just as quickly, culminating in the notorious awkwardness of the morning after. Following a night of spontaneous intimacy, the hesitant kiss on the cheek in the morning lays bare the absurdity of modern love: The closeness of mere hours before dissolves, revealing nothing more than two strangers who briefly intersected. This dynamic is metonymic for other forms of romantic love in the contemporary, shaped by fleeting, commodified desire within capitalist culture. The sociologist Eva Illouz conceptualizes the term "unloving" as a hallmark of this culture, defining it as the dissolution of emotional bonds—when "the one who kept us awake at night now leaves us indifferent" or when we "hurry away from those who excited us a few months ago or even a few hours ago."[1]

Unloving signifies the rapid obsolescence of romantic encounters, which is deeply intertwined with the commodification of the beloved, a central theme throughout

Illouz's oeuvre. In the section of her book on unloving, titled "Beauty as Obsolescence," Illouz shows how this objectification of the beloved entails exerting power and control by ascribing fleeting, diminished value to beauty.[2] Her research interviews illustrate how sexuality is defined today by a built-in logic of obsolescence, where youth and physical appearance, much like the ephemeral aura of disposable commodities, are subject to relentless cycles of devaluation, thus fueling the perpetual drive for aesthetic self-improvement to maintain desirability. In this framework, subjectivity is constructed through both the pursuit and rejection of desire, as relationships are navigated with the same disposable logic that governs consumer behavior—partners are cycled through as swiftly as products, with selfhood asserted by undoing commitments and severing ties.

What is of interest in the context of obsolescence is not unloving per se but rather the persistence of old flames—the unloved—that linger within the fabric of daily life. These are the obsolete "exes"—a term scarcely common before present conceptions of romantic relationships—who continue to haunt us, serving as reminders of past versions of ourselves, refusing to be neatly discarded and to vanish entirely. The one-night stand, in this sense, mirrors the nature of consumer goods, generating a chain of lingering, obsolete lovers—remnants of past passions that awkwardly resurface in unexpected encounters. In *Time Regained*, the final volume of Proust's *In Search of Lost Time*, the narrator reflects on fading infatuations. During a *matinée* at the Guermantes, he observes his past acquaintances and contemplates their transformation in time. Encountering his former love Gilberte, he reacts with surprising indifference. He admits:

> In the past the fear of being no longer myself was something that had terrified me, and this had made

> me dread the end of each new love that I had experienced (for Gilberte, for Albertine), because I could not bear the idea that the "I" who loved them would one day cease to exist, since this in itself would be a kind of death. But by dint of repetition this fear had gradually been transformed into a calm confidence. So that if in those early days, as we have seen, the idea of death had cast a shadow over my loves, for a long time now the remembrance of love had helped me not to fear death. For I realised that dying was not something new, but that on the contrary since my childhood I had already died many times.[3]

Every love, Proust suggests, ends with the death of a loving self. The shift from intimacy to estrangement requires acknowledging a rupture within oneself: a small death and a new beginning. This duplication of the self—created by the disposable orientation of modern temporality—echoes the themes of an earlier chapter, where we explored outdated selves lingering in diaries and VHS tapes. The one-night stand becomes a threshold to broader questions of love, finitude, and disposability, mirroring Proust's insight: a loving self dies, replaced by an indifferent one. Yet while the commodification of relationships parallels the ephemeral nature of fad objects, Proust hints at potential paths to reclaim lost selves and revive dormant flames. In *Time Regained*, Proust elevates involuntary memory, art, and literature as means to transcend obsolescence, capturing an essence beyond temporal decay. More subtly, he also highlights practices of collecting and bibliophilia, connecting these to personal memory. The novel's opening, where the narrator's mother reads *François le champi*, returns as a moment of self-resurrection:

> A thing which we saw, a book which we read at a certain period does not merely remain forever

> conjoined to what existed then around us; it remains also faithfully united to what we ourselves then were and thereafter it can be handled only by the sensibility, the personality that were then ours. If, even in thought, I pick from the bookshelf *François le Champi*, immediately there rises within me a child who takes my place, who alone has the right to spell out the title *François le Champi*, and who reads it as he read it once before, with the same impression of what the weather was like then in the garden, the same dreams that were then shaping themselves in his mind about the different countries and about life, the same anguish about the next day.[4]

Collecting offers a strategy for confronting the anguish of lost selves, providing a semblance of control—a way to organize and curate selfhood into a coherent narrative, one in which past selves can be possessed on our own terms. Rather than simply revisiting the awkwardness of obsolete selves, this chapter examines the resistance to their arbitrary lingering through the practice of collecting. In the chapter on the non-image, we explored an aesthetic form defined by its relationship to the cycle of accelerated obsolescence. Now we turn to the collection to see how loving encounters are negotiated in relation to their already acknowledged fate as obsolete. Commodities, when transformed into collectors' items, evade their obsolescence, just as love—fantasized as eternal—seeks to escape dissolution through the logic of collection.

According to Benjamin, the collector's desire is not only to transcend the functionality of the collected object; rather, the collector "takes up the struggle against dispersion."[5] By arranging a collection signifying totality, the "great collector is struck by the confusion, by the scatter, in which the things of the world are found."[6] Marcel's break with Albertine exemplifies the pains of dispersion for the possessive lover not only of objects but also of the loved one encapsulated in them. When Albertine leaves him suddenly, Marcel admits that the objects containing her traces seem to be "seeking to give me a translation, a different version, for a second time to tell me, of her departure," while the objects around the house, the armchair in which he used to sit in the company of Albertine, trigger the "innumerable and humbler 'selves' that compose our personality which was still unaware of Albertine's departure and must be informed of it."[7] The fleeting presence of Albertine and the delayed communication through letters are unbearable for Marcel, much like the dispersed objects that cruelly remind him of her absence.

If, within a system of unloving, power is exerted through the objectification of the beloved, collecting emerges as a strategy to mediate this power by transforming the ephemeral value of the beloved-as-commodity into the enduring continuity of the collection. The protagonists of Orhan Pamuk's novel *The Museum of Innocence*, Michel Gondry's film *Eternal Sunshine of the Spotless Mind*, and Nick Hornby's novel *High Fidelity* (subsequently adapted into a film and a television series), all at the center of this chapter, manipulate objects to counter the dispersion of both material things and love-objects in order to ultimately safeguard their selves unchanged. Their narratives illuminate not only the act of collecting as a material manipulation of obsolete things but also the perception of love itself—something seemingly ephemeral, fated for obsolescence.

Collecting shows how the loss experienced in the dissolution of love is ultimately a loss of self—a mourning for the person we once were during that love. In the loving encounter, through the eyes of the stranger in front of us, we see *ourselves* as objects of desire. We imagine a future for this phantasmatic self and, then, when the morning arrives and we are unloved, mourn for having lost this discarded future. We mourn for a virtual version of ourselves who, by dying, assures us that they must have lived. These are the selves encapsulated in the armchair and the objects dispersed in the house: not only the traces of Albertine but of Marcel, the one that was defined in the eyes of Albertine.

It is not the obsolescence of the loved one that holds paramount importance but the narcissistic mourning of the collector—here, predominantly a masculine and possessive form of mourning—for his own lost self. By organizing and collecting objects, the protagonists I examine attempt to construct a coherent self—both their own and that of their lovers—rendering them reachable and controllable. Unlike the nonimage, which is defined by its obsolescence yet remains light enough to invite multiple misreadings, the collection seeks to immunize itself against subversive future interpretations. Collecting is not merely about preserving love from melancholic fading; it is also about controlling how the encounter is narrated and reproduced.

Collecting Füsun

The Museum of Innocence unfolds against the backdrop of 1970s Istanbul, a period during which Turkey's upper class grapples with the juxtaposition of traditional values and the influences of Western consumerism. The narrative is presented through the lens of Kemal, a businessman who is soon to marry Sibel, both coming from affluent and esteemed families. The story begins with Kemal's purchase of a handbag for his fiancée from a lavish Western store, where he encounters Füsun, a distant relative employed there. This chance meeting sets in motion a tumultuous love affair and infatuation between Kemal and Füsun, with the reenchantment of objects and material remnants playing a pivotal role in their story.

At the novel's outset, two distinct categories of objects come to the forefront. On one hand, there is the realm of commodities, exemplified by the opulent handbag Kemal acquires for Sibel and by the introduction of Turkey's "first fruit soda" by one of Kemal's acquaintances.[8] On the other hand, there are objects that Kemal associates with Füsun and their shared experiences—everyday items like earrings, cigarette stubs, matchsticks, and other mundane articles imbued with tangible or symbolic traces of Füsun herself. Throughout the course of their love affair, Kemal collects these objects, almost as if he anticipates the tragic turn of events that ultimately unfolds with Füsun's death in a car accident.

Kemal's desire for Füsun reflects Aristophanes's myth from Plato's *Symposium*, a long-standing meditation on the nature of love. Aristophanes explains the origin of love through a celestial myth: Once there were three sexes—male, female, and a union of both, who were complete in their duality. This third sex was so powerful in its completeness that it turned against the gods, and Zeus punished them by splitting them into halves. Love, then, became the perpetual search for one's missing half, a desire to restore the completeness lost in the divine schism. In Aristophanes's words:

> So it is that from that far back in time love of one another has been innate in human beings and is what restores our old natural state and attempts to make one out of two and to heal our human nature. Thus each of us is a token of a human being in as much as he has been split like a flatfish, two out of one. Each is then constantly looking for his matching token.[9]

The Aristophanist conception of love is inherently belated—forever chasing after something lost. It introduces a certain temporality of love: Love is not merely an event but a final, total experience, inseparable from the idea of finitude.

Through this lens, the love encounter, in its attempt to recover a lost unity, becomes a means to reverse the afterlife of this unity itself, which once existed but has now become irrelevant. In this sense, love and death are closely intertwined; merging with another involves a transformation into something new, a complete and irreversible state. However, as Illouz's work suggests, love encounters in late modernity often unfold as a series of ad hoc unities, each transient and ephemeral. A sense of disposability prevails, where love, like a commodity, is consumed and exhausted almost instantly—attained and immediately abandoned. This accelerated cycle of love and loss offers a timely reinterpretation of the Aristophanic myth, in which the original temporality of belatedness is now bound to the cyclical rhythms of a consumerist world perpetually striving for the new.

In *The Museum of Innocence*, the Aristophanist wish of merging is manifested through its perpetual delay. Kemal suffers from Füsun's ungraspable presence, even after the "one instant of perfect happiness" when the two were physically "one" in their lovemaking.[10] When Füsun decides to end their affair, the narrator indulges in long descriptions of his agony as he waits for her at the Merhamet Apartments, where they used to meet. When Füsun fails to appear, objects serve as a "palliative cure":

> Eight to ten minutes later I was lying on the bed at the Merhamet Apartments, trying to pick up Füsun's scent in the sheets, and it was almost as if I was trying to feel her inside me, almost as if I wanted to become her, but her scent had grown fainter. With all the strength I could muster, I embraced the sheets and then reached out to pick up the glass paperweight on the table, desperate for traces of the scent of her hands. As I inhaled deeply from the glass, I felt

> instant relief in my nose, my lungs. I lay there holding and sniffing the paperweight, for I don't know how long. According to calculations made later from memory, I had given her this paperweight on June 2, as a present, and as with so many other presents I gave her, she, not wishing to arouse her mother's suspicions, elected not to take it home.[11]

Seemingly, Kemal's yearning to fuse with Füsun is clear, as he expresses a desire to "become her." Yet Füsun's presence is unreliable, fleeting, and increasingly inaccessible. Objects like the sheets and the paperweight become repositories of memory and desire, providing Kemal with refuge as he clings to physical remnants. These objects, carefully categorized and associated with specific dates and moments, form the foundation of the Museum of Innocence, a museum that materializes both in the novel and in Pamuk's real-world museum in Istanbul, opened in 2012.[12]

While Kemal's compulsion to collect seems to be a way of controlling Füsun's presence and guarding against her ephemeral nature, it also signifies a reluctance to fully merge with her in the present. His collection freezes her in time, maintaining an untimely distance between them. Paradoxically, the very act of preserving her essence through objects distances Kemal from Füsun, preventing a true merging that could risk losing control over her presence. The cigarette stub is a prime example of this inversion. A cigarette, inherently ephemeral, burns and perishes like an hourglass. Kemal collects 4,213 of Füsun's cigarette stubs, reflecting the obsessive totality of his desire—no object can "escape" or scatter.[13] The stub becomes a materialized embodiment of the distance Kemal wishes to manipulate in order to hold onto Füsun:

> Beside my head was the side table on which she had left her watch so carefully the first two times we

> made love. For a week, I had been aware that in the ashtray now resting there was the butt of cigarette Füsun had stubbed out. At one moment I picked it up, breathing in its scent of smoke and ash, and placing it between my lips. I was about to light it (imagining perhaps for a moment that by loving her so, I had become her), but I realized that if I did so there would be nothing left of the relic.[14]

Kemal's reflection on Füsun's cigarette stub is pivotal to understanding his collector's logic. Earlier, collecting was proposed as a way to counteract obsolescence—a method to control the temporality of consumption by transferring an object into an alternative sphere, where it interacts with other objects under a defined theme. The moment with the cigarette stub reveals that Kemal does not wish to simply *consume* Füsun nor to fuse with her as the Aristophanist would have it ("I had become her"); this would entail a consumption of both individuals into a single entity. Instead, he prefers to collect Füsun—metonymically through the cigarette stub—in a manner that leaves him with a perpetual sense of control. This control, as we will now see, is not over Füsun herself but over time and its inevitable effects on both people and material objects.

Material Narration

John Elsner and Roger Cardinal posit that collectors are propelled by a narcissistic desire not only to own a specific category of items but also to possess, in a sense, the entire universe, evinced in their insistence on the completeness of the collection.[15] Building on a parallel idea, Krzysztof Pomian illustrates how this desire has characterized individual collections (known as *collections particulières* in his terms) throughout history, dating back to the origins of the cabinet of curiosities

(*Wunderkammer*) in early modern Europe.[16] Pomian demonstrates that early modern curiosities were often curated around totalizing themes, such as the four elements or the four seasons. These collections were metonymic of a desire to exert total control over the world by amassing both natural and artificial curiosities from various corners of the globe. In the postindustrial context, particularly in the early works of Jean Baudrillard, a collector's possession mainly contrasts with the notions of use or functionality. The possessive desire becomes evident when the object is abstracted from its practical functions, leaving behind a pure yearning for ownership.[17]

In Kemal's case, the yearning for total possession is centered on Füsun. His meticulous collecting and archiving are imbued with a desire not merely to possess random objects but to materialize and, by extension, possess the evanescent presence of his beloved. For Kemal, these objects cease to function merely as commodities; even stained playing cards or stubbed cigarettes become valuable artifacts, significant insofar as they trigger memories of Füsun. While Kemal's collection ostensibly appears to be dedicated to preserving the memory of Füsun, the objects—and the idealized vision of Füsun etched onto them—remain subject to his personal desire for singularity. The objects encapsulate not just the memory of Füsun but also reflect Kemal's desire for a unique and singular narrative. In this light, the collection becomes a vessel for Kemal's own longing and introspection, raising the question of whether his pursuit is more about mourning the loss of Füsun or mourning the alterations within himself.

In Baudrillard's *The System of Objects*, collecting is explicitly linked to self-mourning. According to Baudrillard, the collector does not merely defy death or finitude by preserving material traces of themselves through objects, assuming that the objects endow them with a "life after death." Rather, it is the very essence of collecting—establishing an alternative timeline over which the collector maintains control—that enables them to engage in a process of self-mourning.[18] Through collecting, which allows for the illusion of controlling both time and the narrative of the self, the collector mourns for their own impending death while still alive.

The Museum of Innocence is haunted, from the beginning, by this sense of posterity and mourning. Even before the reader learns about the future Museum of Innocence, Kemal narrates as if he is already preparing these objects for display, preserving them for a future audience. He frequently refers to objects in the past tense, as if describing exhibits from his own life: "Now, years later … I am exhibiting here an illustrated menu, an advertisement, a matchbook, and a napkin from Fuaye"[19] or "I have here the clock, and these matchsticks and matchbooks, because the display suggests how I spent the slow ten or fifteen minutes it took to accept that Füsun was not coming that day."[20] Kemal's encounter with Füsun is inseparable from this posterity, with both he and the reader mourning the affair as if it were already over before it began.

This feeling of mourning is intensified by the juxtaposition of literary and material narratives. In fact, the very first sentence in the novel is one of posterior reflection: "It was the happiest moment of my life, though I didn't know it."[21] This is, as mentioned, aligned with the accumulation of objects and the opening of the collection to the public, which is focused on the same need for both literary and material self-narration. After being released from the hospital, following the accident in which Füsun has died, Kemal first thinks about opening his collection: "A feeling awoke in me that if I could tell my story I could ease my pain."[22] Later, even more explicitly, he admits: "I would imagine it possible for me to frame my collection with a story, and I would dream happily of a museum where I could display my life."[23] The collection, and the novel's narrative of it, are both charged with the narcissistic desire to create a literary-material embodiment of the fantasied image of the self.

Toward the end of the novel, Kemal realizes that sharing his story may involve dispossession from its modes of articulation, not only in that he displays his collection "out in the open." He also asks Orhan Pamuk, in an inside-narrative appearance, to tell his story to the readers. The novel, seemingly, is narrated by Pamuk, who uses the first-person singular to narrate the story as Kemal, a metanarrative reenactment of actual enmeshments between author and character: "I am speaking in your voice. Right now I am trying very hard to put myself in your place, to be you," Pamuk says to Kemal. Inside the narrative, Kemal's decision to allow Pamuk to tell history is a crack in the singularity Kemal insisted so fervently to maintain.[24]

Alongside the profanation of narration comes an attempt to profane the collection. After numerous visits to museums worldwide, including a trip to Proust's Illiers-Combray, Kemal decides to transform his private collection into a public museum. This shift signifies more than just sharing his story and displaying the objects to strangers; it also involves the acquisition of items from other collectors across the globe. The objects Kemal purchases in flea markets in Athens and Rome bear a striking resemblance to or are identical to the ones associated with Füsun. In this sense, Kemal not only allows others to narrate his story but also permits others' objects to contribute to this narrative. The act of purchasing objects from different collectors represents a departure from the exclusive, singular narrative Kemal initially sought to maintain, expanding the scope of the collection and introducing new voices and perspectives into the narrative.

However, the movement toward dispossession is not total. For him, there are two types of collectors: the proud and the bashful. While the first "regard the museum as a natural ultimate destination for their collections," the second collect "purely for the sake of collecting."[25] Interestingly, Kemal associates himself with the bashful type; he collects "in pursuit of an answer" or as a "palliative for a pain."[26] Given this fact, perhaps, the Museum of Innocence is an ambivalent space for display, in which some possessive sentimentality remains nevertheless. Kemal says that

> when visitors to our museum view these objects, they should feel respect for my love and compare it with memories of their own. The premises should never be crowded, so that the visitor can examine unhurried each object, and view the pictures of the Istanbul neighborhoods we visited hand in hand, getting a leisurely feel for that entire collection as a totality.[27]

The museum affords Kemal the same logic of the cigarette butt, the material remainder that he keeps as his personal insurance. While museums typically function as spaces and institutions for displaying objects, they inherently maintain a distance between the exhibited items and the spectators. Objects are presented publicly precisely because they are preserved and well kept. In the Museum of Innocence, what stands out most prominently is Kemal's insistence on living inside it. Despite his mother's advice, he chooses to spend his nights in the attic of the museum's space: "What could be more beautiful than to spend one's nights surrounded by objects connecting one to his deepest sentimental attachments and memories!"[28] Both symbolically and materially the Museum of Innocence freezes the image of Füsun so that time can be manipulated under the possession and control of Kemal. By no coincidence, he urges Pamuk's character in the last sentence of the novel to "let everyone know, I lived a very happy life."[29]

The Museum of Innocence primarily functions therefore as a museum for Kemal, where he himself becomes an artifact within its confines. Kemal, experiencing the present infatuation with Füsun as already a memory to mourn for, has always been an artifact. His affair with Füsun was perceived and manipulated as an artifact even as it unfolded. The Museum of Innocence, with Kemal as an artifact within it, stands as a monumental exhibit showcasing a complete and meticulously narrated self. In his quest for a life worth remembering, Kemal imposed a forced inertia on both Füsun and himself, relegating them to the status of museum artifacts. The museum, in essence, solidifies and finalizes this position. The true profanation, if any, occurs in the external Museum of Innocence established by Pamuk in Istanbul. By associating himself with a public museum and relinquishing control over the very narrative of his affair, Pamuk enacts the final dispossession.

Füsun was destined to fade like an obsolete commodity. Yet precisely because collecting preserves commodities by detaching them from the cycle of consumption, Kemal attempts to collect Füsun to prevent her dissolution into obsolescence. His collection serves as a form of material mourning, securing a trace of her that remains under his control, shielding their love from the inevitable forces of time and finitude. However, this very act undermines his pursuit of an Aristophanic love—a total merging with the other that risks vanishing without leaving a remainder for consolation. Unlike the fleeting nature of a one-night stand, Kemal preemptively safeguards his love encounter, unwilling to let it dissolve into memory. Aware of the Proustian realization that love is finite, bound to a perpetual cycle of death and resurrection, his collection exerts control not only over Füsun but also over the narrative of his own self. Unlike Marcel, who must suffer the dispersal of Albertine's absence, Kemal's museum ensures that neither Füsun nor he will undergo the same fate.

Voluntary Forgetting

The protagonists of *Eternal Sunshine of the Spotless Mind*, the 2004 film directed by Michel Gondry and written by Charlie Kaufman, take an approach entirely opposite to that of Kemal.[30] In the film, Joel (Jim Carrey) and Clementine (Kate Winslet), whose relationship begins with a spark but eventually deteriorates, choose to erase each other from their memories. The film vividly illustrates a condition that materializes Illouz's commentary on unloving in its most straightforward sense: Joel and Clementine refuse to be "exes," burdened by the lingering memory of a faded romance. Instead, they opt to dispose of their relationship, much like everyday waste, casting it into a neglected realm of oblivion.

In the fictional company Lacuna, Joel is instructed to gather all the objects that remind him of Clementine. If Kemal collects Füsun to memorialize their love, the universe of *Eternal Sunshine* presents a parallel act of deliberate amnesia. Through the materiality of photographs, custom-made mugs, and gifts for Clementine, Lacuna constructs a map of memories to be erased. Each object associated with Clementine, gathered to be discarded or "decollected," serves as a tool to locate and isolate the memories tied to it. Joel's process materializes Marcel's approach in *In Search of Lost Time*, albeit differently. Marcel "tells" each object tied to Albertine that she is gone, acknowledging their shared history even as he mourns its loss. Joel avoids this painful confrontation with memory, actively collecting the possessions associated with Clementine in order to avoid "telling" them that she is gone, finding refuge in their immediate disposal. In doing so, Joel effectively denies the agonies of transition, annihilating the version of himself linked to Clementine and choosing erasure over a reconciliation imbued with melancholy.

The interplay of selfhood, love, and objects lies at the heart of the film. Joel's decision to erase Clementine comes after he meets her in the bookshop where she works, only to discover that she no longer remembers him and treats him as a complete stranger. This logic—akin to that of a one-night stand, where extreme intimacy quickly turns into cold detachment—proves unbearable for Joel. Like Clementine, he decides that erasing the "self" imbued with the memory of an old flame is preferable to mourning its loss. Similarly, Clementine explains to Lacuna that she wants to erase Joel because he has "changed her" so profoundly that she no longer feels like herself. The tension between an intense love encounter and its immediate disposal creates, as Marcel anticipated, an unloving that necessarily entails self-mourning—a finality that signifies the violent dissolution of a transient self.

Here, too, the emergence and finitude of the loving self are entangled with memories materialized in objects. In *Eternal Sunshine*, Patrick, an employee at Lacuna who falls in love with Clementine, uses the objects collected by Joel to attract her. Rather than discarding these items, Patrick reclaims them—objects now abandoned by their original possessor—and gives Clementine the very gifts that Joel had initially given to her. When Joel discovers this, he angrily accuses Patrick of stealing "his" belongings and, by extension, "his" identity. What is fascinating, however, is that Patrick's theft involves objects that Joel had already rejected, tied to a self that Joel had consciously chosen to discard. In relinquishing Clementine and the collector's identity embodied in these objects, Joel had already disposed of the version of himself he now claims Patrick has stolen.

Eternal Sunshine resonates with the theme of voluntary memory through its apparent counterpoint: voluntary forgetting. If the dès vu, as the culmination of desperate, voluntary memory, has been associated with the introduction (and obsolescence) of the photographic medium, in *Eternal Sunshine* the mind becomes akin to a VHS tape—capable of erasure and rerecording overlapping material. However, voluntary forgetting in the film is confronted by the bugs inherent to technology itself. Not only do Joel and Clementine leave involuntary emotional remnants within each other, but they also find ways to resist the erasure process as it unfolds within Joel's mind. By choosing to "mix" memories and take refuge in experiences they never actually shared, they engage in a dynamic, fluid form of remembrance that aligns more closely with the Bergsonian virtual than with the already actualized logic of technological inscription.

In a system of disposable partners and lingering exes, Clementine and Joel ultimately choose to bear the consequences of obsolete selves and fading infatuations. The film reveals that the opening scene—Joel and Clementine's chance encounter on a train—does not precede their memory erasure but follows it. After unknowingly rekindling a flame, they gradually uncover their shared past. Clementine listens to Joel's Lacuna recording, where he harshly lists the things he dislikes about her. Yet, against the imperative of their past, the film concludes with Joel and Clementine, as amnesiac strangers, choosing to try again. Rather than mourning the loss of their initial spark, they embrace the reality that love, though it may fade, can endure.

This entanglement of love and finitude echoes the film's title, drawn from Alexander Pope's poem on the celebrated yet tragic love affair of Abelard and Heloise. The "eternal sunshine" signifies an infinite clarity, free of beginnings and ends, expectations and disappointments—akin to the bliss of erasing an old flame from one's memory. Written from Heloise's perspective, Pope's poem ("Eloisa to Abelard") portrays her lingering love as a hopeless yet enduring flame:

"Ah hopeless, lasting flames! like those that burn/To light the dead, and warm th' unfruitful urn."[31] This flame, tied to loss and unfruitfulness, persists in conditions where love is rendered impossible, as in the case of Heloise and Abelard. For Clementine and Joel, however, the lingering flame becomes the remnant that endures beyond their desire for a spotless mind. By embracing this lasting love, they accept finitude and the "death of selves" as integral to a long-term love story—one shaped by enduring embers rather than fleeting sparks and sudden cooldowns.

Multiple Deaths

If Kemal collects material traces of his singular beloved in *The Museum of Innocence* and Joel and Clementine "decollect" them in *Eternal Sunshine of the Spotless Mind*, then in *High Fidelity*, it is not the beloved but rather the unloved—the mythological exes—who are meticulously collected. Nick Hornby's novel (1995), later adapted into a film starring John Cusack (2000) and a Hulu series starring Zoë Kravitz (2020), intertwines the world of record collecting with the presentist conditions of love and unloving, accumulating exes who haunt the present as past promises.[32] I turn now to *High Fidelity* to juxtapose the drama of erasing an old flame with that of collecting it—two different forms of amnesia, each imposing a controlled curation of the self and of objects to avoid confronting an obsolete self and lover. The trajectory from Kemal (who collects to idealize) to Joel and Clementine (who decollect to forget) culminates in *High Fidelity*, where the collection does not strive to preserve a singular love but instead curates a series of breakups—scattered across time like lingering, unresolved flames.

High Fidelity (referring primarily to the novel and 2000 film, since the Hulu series diverges significantly from the original narrative) is narrated by Rob, the owner of the record shop Revolver. The story begins with Rob's breakup with Laura. The heartbroken narrator, still in denial, lists his "top five exes," as though heartbreak could be managed by cataloging past relationships. As the narrative unfolds through this list—from a first awkward kiss after school to an intimidatingly intelligent college ex—the exes become a personal, sentimental collection. Each relationship is anchored to a distinct phase of Rob's life, akin to records cataloged and shelved. The comparison between romantic relationships and a curated collection reflects a thematic connection between collecting and navigating transient love.

This aligns with *High Fidelity*'s broader themes of listing, collecting, and taste. Rob and his employees frequently compile top-five lists—from the best Dustin Hoffman films to songs recorded by blind musicians. Collecting, particularly the self-definition and social distinction achieved through consuming commodities, becomes a lens through which the characters are understood. Dick, an employee at Revolver, is initially portrayed by the narrator as someone who "wears a Sonic Youth T-shirt," reads a "paperback biography of Lou Reed," and carries a bag that "advertises a violently fashionable American independent record label."[33] Barry (played by Jack Black in the film) refuses to sell a Stevie Wonder record to a middle-aged customer, deeming it "bad taste."

For Rob, listing, collecting, and curating provide a means to sustain a coherent and unchanging sense of self. Unlike with Marcel, where encountering a former love signals the death of a past self, Rob's obsessive cataloging helps him stabilize his identity, avoiding internal contradictions. After his breakup with Laura, he reorganizes his record collection in autobiographical order—arranging records according to when he acquired them. Baudrillard's notion of collecting as self-mourning is particularly relevant here: Rob's collection becomes his own "museum of innocence." As Rob puts it:

> That way I hope to write my own autobiography, without having to do anything like pick up a pen. I pull the records off the shelves, put them in piles all over the sitting room floor, look for *Revolver*, and go on from there, and when I've finished I'm flushed with a sense of self, because this, after all, is who I am.[34]

Rob does not just revisit his collection; he also revisits his exes. His list of top-five exes becomes a way for him to reflect on his romantic failures. Here, his collecting mirrors Benjamin's notion of dispersion—Rob can't tolerate arbitrariness in his life, whether it concerns movies, songs, or ex-lovers. His meticulous organization reflects an attempt to control not only cultural artifacts but, by extension, time itself.

Unlike the organization of the already tamed collection, the meetings with his exes are more troubling—particularly the meeting with the intelligent and fashionable Charlie, the one who was always "out of his league" and with whom he always felt like an imposter doomed to exposure. The meeting with present-day Charlie, both in the novel and in the book, is revelatory. Charlie is still cool, she still hangs out with her bohemian friends at bourgeois dinner parties, but now all the magic has dissipated. Rob leaves the dinner party disenchanted, realizing that her tendency of "not listening" to others once mistaken for her strength of character and the obtuseness once "misread as a mystery" are now evident flaws.[35]

Rob's fantasy about his past and the way it shaped his present identity faces a challenge with the encounter with Charlie. Instead of being possessed by his past self, and unable to sustain the fantasy any longer, Rob comes to the realization that this past self is already dead. In his perception, Charlie has remained the same, prompting him to recognize that it is he who has unexpectedly changed, transcending the linear boundaries narrated by his record collection. This encounter with Charlie forces Rob to confront the fluidity and unpredictability of personal transformation, challenging the notion of a fixed and curated identity that he has attempted to maintain through the evolution of his musical taste. Rob's disenchantment with Charlie, much like the loss of allure in a commodity over time, becomes an experience of liberation.

When Laura's dad dies and Rob is called to the funeral, the latter encounters his own neglected angst of finitude: "What happened to me during the funeral was something like this: I saw, for the first time, how scared I am of dying, and of other people dying and how this fear has prevented me from doing all sorts of things."[36] Yet, similar to Kemal, Rob isn't simply afraid of death as the ultimate end; his are fears of becoming someone else, of the death of a self that once possessed the most fashionable punk records and now, as a typical settled bourgeoisie, seems unworthy of owning them. In this sense, one of the significant things that this specific fear of death has prevented Rob from pursuing is a long monogamous relationship. When meeting an attractive journalist for an interview after rekindling with Laura, Rob is tempted to revert to his habitual fantasies, "imagining in tiny detail the entire course of the relationship, from the first kiss, to bed, to moving in together, to getting married."[37] Yet this is, after all, the fantasy of the present Rob: a fantasy that primarily signifies his need to preserve himself in the unexpected future.

What truly troubles Rob is the passage of time—the way both love and the selves bound to it slip into obsolescence, dissolving into scattered remnants rather than remaining safeguarded within the curated continuity of a collection. Both the novel and film versions of *High Fidelity* conclude with Rob choosing to settle down with Laura, even though he knows he will "never spend two or three days in a sweat trying to remember what she looks like. Never again will I get to a pub half an hour early to meet her, staring at the same article in a magazine and looking at my watch every thirty seconds."[38] On the surface, this follows the conventional romantic-comedy arc of "growing up," but Rob's transformation also signals a deeper acceptance of time's effects. By ending his endless pursuit of novelty—those first kisses and newly sparked flames—he embraces the inevitability of obsolescence: the aging and dying of a self, yet also a love that endures.

In the final scene, Rob transcends his self-absorbed image by creating a mixtape not as a projection of his own taste but as a gift of songs Laura—and not necessarily he—would enjoy. This gesture marks a shift, as the mixtape itself encapsulates the essence of collection. Earlier, Rob explains the meticulous art of curating a mixtape, stressing how each song must be carefully chosen and perfectly ordered. Until this moment, his mixtapes served as exhibitions of his musical persona, a collector controlling the narrative of his life. Creating a mixtape for Laura marks a surrender of control—collecting *for* her rather than collecting *her* becomes a profound acceptance of the inevitable loss inherent in finitude. It is a willingness to embrace a love that fades, deteriorates, and persists nonetheless.

For Kemal, Joel, Clementine, and Rob, collecting functions as a shield against love's transience—because it is, ultimately, a shield against the self's transience when entangled with fleeting love encounters. Each character resists the ephemerality of love, where anything beyond the idealized first kiss risks exhaustion and obsolescence. They safeguard and idealize moments, selectively imposing amnesia on others. Kemal of *The Museum of Innocence* clings to a static self because that self possesses Füsun; his identity remains frozen within the museum, protected from dispersion. In contrast, *Eternal Sunshine of the Spotless Mind* dismantles the collector's impulse to arrest time, offering instead a cyclical return to love despite its inevitable dissolution. For *High Fidelity*'s Rob, committing to a long-term relationship means confronting a world of outdated has-beens, where former "cool" kids now chase their children through suburban neighborhoods. Drawing on Proust's poetics, these characters collect and uncollect in an effort to avoid "dying"—that is, changing in response to their love objects and risking the becoming of other selves, like future versions cringing at their past selves on VHS tapes. They strive to remain fixed, curating their biographies rather than acknowledging them as fluid and continually unfolding.

Yet Rob's epiphany need not signify a descent into the mundane stagnation of adulthood. By ceasing his pursuit of perpetual "newness," he discovers a love that persists in life rather than in inertia or death. This invites a return to Aristophanes's myth of love, at least as it is reframed through the economy of unloving—a temporality of love that culminates in a singular, irrevocable act of merging. This temporality, which in the cases studied has been intertwined with masculine idealization and control, knows only two extremes: burning or vanishing. It cannot endure as a fading flame.

All the while, as we have seen, love can scarcely survive within the curated structure of the collection, where its flame is suffocated by predictability. The collection transforms love into a mirror of the (often masculine) collector, rather than a genuine encounter with another. In contrast, Rob's conclusion offers a different possibility: love as a flame that flickers but does not extinguish—not because it is protected from obsolescence but because it is allowed to age and to become obsolete, bearing the risk of duration rather than being discarded and negated altogether.

4
Postindustrial Ragpicking

In nineteenth-century Paris, when the night fell on the city of lights at the end of a busy day, it was more than probable that pedestrians encountered ragpickers in the street: men whose job was to pick through the leftovers of textile manufacturing and return rags, odds, and ends to the industrial chain, mostly for the benefit of the paper industry. Although *chiffons*—the word refers to "cloths" or "rags"—had been used to manufacture paper since the Middle Ages, the Industrial Revolution created an insatiable demand for them in France between 1830 and 1870.[1] Until the end of the nineteenth century, when the paper industry started to rely on wood and *poubelles* appeared on street corners as containers for litter, ragpicking was not only possible but at times even a decent way to make a living.[2] Approximately six thousand *chiffoniers* (and some *chiffonnières* too) were registered in the city's books; they earned between eighteen and forty-four francs for one hundred kilograms of chiffons, depending on their quality.[3]

The ragpicker is a familiar figure in nineteenth-century fiction and poetry. It appears amid the *misérables* of the city in works by Victor Hugo and Baudelaire. Baudelaire, in "The Ragman's Wine," writes that the ragpicker "staggers against the walls, as poets do."[4] He establishes a bond between the ragpicker and the poet not only because the rags that were picked would eventually become the paper upon which a poem was printed but also because both the ragpicker and the poet sacrifice their individuality to blend into the urban crowd and experience the industrial city at its utmost intensity. In "The Ragman's Wine," the load of debris that the ragpicker carries is likened to the jumbled vomit of Paris.[5] Both the ragpicker and the poet, as Baudelaire suggests, bear the responsibility of engaging with the defunct, in which they find a potential for novelty.

The tradition of *chiffonnage* is grounded in the industrial conditions of the nineteenth century, together with parallel figures such as the *flâneur*. However, while the flâneur is impulsive and spontaneous, the ragpicker is methodical and "implacable."[6] According to Marc Berdet, Benjamin's unfinished work, the *Passagenwerk*, manifests a thinking that is already more inclined toward the figure of the ragpicker than the flâneur. For Benjamin as for Berdet, the ragpicker is a figure at once inside and outside society, as they examine the "phantasmagorias," the collective unconscious fantasies of a newly capitalist and bourgeois society, through unremitting work amid its obsolete objects and debris.[7]

In the postindustrial economy, the rise of disposability, epitomized by plastics, has supplanted the culture of reuse that once defined ragpicking. If ragpicking has become less visible in the postindustrial city, it is because this city is governed by the regime of simulacra, presenting production itself as already obsolete and thereby obscuring its material traces, decay, and residues. What becomes of the bond between the writer and the ragpicker in an economy where materiality is denied yet disposability is accelerated? How does the figure of the ragpicker reflect not only a transformation of practice but also gesture toward the subjective dispossession found in writing itself? This chapter centers on Annie Ernaux's literary practice as a form of postindustrial ragpicking—one that unfolds both through urban residues and through the subjective salvaging of estranged memories. Ernaux's work introduces a form of literary ragpicking that registers dispossession as both urban and personal. Her writing becomes a striking case study because, as I will show, its mode of subjective dispossession through writing becomes the very condition for her attunement to the obsolete: to the objects, people, and memories swiftly discarded within a culture of accelerated novelty.

While Baudelaire's association with ragpicking is tied to the materiality of the modern city—the center of capitalist production—Ernaux's ragpicking attends to the postindustrial urban condition, in which the city is codified and privatized and conforms to a presentist fantasy of seamless, decay-free temporality. I read Ernaux alongside a broader transformation of postindustrial urban space, particularly in New York City, where public life has been increasingly sanitized, privatized, and emptied of the tactile remains that once made ragpicking possible. Works such as John Wilson's series *How To* and the documentary *Redemption* help frame a cultural shift in which waste does not disappear but instead changes its modes of visibility.

Whereas the previous chapter explored collecting as a curatorial negotiation of obsolescence—through which the self is stabilized and shaped—ragpicking introduces a different register. It shifts the focus from private curation to the collective and material dimensions of cultural memory, offering a mode of understanding culture through its residues. To step into the practice of ragpicking is to recognize that an insistence on the obsolete is inseparable from an occupation of the urban commons. Though often considered an obsolete practice, ragpicking persists in multiple forms—countering the sterility of postindustrial urban space and reembedding it with the potential for transformation by reinserting it into time. As a material practice, ragpicking underscores the transformative and reappropriative power of the discarded, offering a counterarchive to a culture that would rather forget what it no longer needs.

Mnemonic Chiffonnage

Ernaux's literary works are entrenched in a reality of an ongoing acceleration of the discarding of the old and the purchasing (and discarding) of the new, along with a denial of the aged and the obsolete that affects objects and human beings alike. The two main thematic strands of Ernaux's oeuvre, the strand of reminiscence (manifested in *The Years* and *A Girl's Story*) and the strand of the urban diary (*Exteriors*, *Things Seen*, and *Look at the Lights My Love*), are intertwined in a move toward a poetics of chiffonnage. Much like the correlation between the ragpicker's métier and the poet's that Baudelaire notices, Ernaux finds a poetic mechanism that turns residues into writing in order to preserve and repurpose outdated objects, memories, and people. Without explicitly referring to ragpicking, Ernaux reconfigures the tradition of chiffonnage within postindustrial conditions and contemporary consumer culture, where commodities are designed vis-à-vis their disposability and ephemerality.

Ernaux's *The Years* (*Les années*), published in 2008, functions as a collective autobiography—an "auto"-biography of a generation. Like Proust in *Time Regained*, Ernaux openly addresses the reader at the end of this work and concludes with observations, again like Proust, on memory and reminiscence. However, Ernaux's account of autobiography, of reminiscence by literary means, is directed toward the impersonality of memory. In her opinion, autobiography cannot simply be written as one's personal possession since memory is essentially collective. It escapes the hold of the seemingly autonomous reminiscent mind:

> Then, in a state of profound, almost dazzling satisfaction, she finds something that the image from personal memory doesn't give her on its own: a kind of vast collective sensation that takes her consciousness, her entire being, into itself. She has the same feeling, alone in the car on the highway, of being taken into the indefinable whole of the world of now, from the closest to the most remote of things."[8]

Later, she will add:

> There is no "I" in what she views as a sort of impersonal autobiography. There is only "one" and "we," as if now it were her turn to tell the story of the time-before.[9]

The Years, written in the impersonal voice "*on*" (and when addressing the narrator herself, the detached "*elle*"), exemplifies this view of the impossibility of pure "auto"-biography. The narrative, oscillating between personal and collective events, intentionally aims to tell the story of an entire generation. In the first pages of the novel, and again when approaching its conclusion, Ernaux enumerates memories arbitrarily (whether images from childhood or TV commercials), interrupting the course of narration, as if she has to inscribe them on paper immediately before letting them vanish into oblivion. From a personal perspective, she explains that she wants to save these memories before she loses her ability to remember.[10] From a collective perspective, she stresses the importance of saving something from a time that will never come back, evidently something wide and encompassing, that is nevertheless inscribed in Ernaux's own personal course of life.[11]

While involuntary memory is in line with the spontaneous strolling of the flâneur, Ernaux's voluntary memory is as methodical and desperate as ragpicking. She insists on residual pieces of memory, negligible as they might seem. Ernaux's tendency toward collective configurations of memory aligns with the ragpicker's position inside and outside society at once, a position that enables her to detect and define collective fantasies:

> We lived in a profusion of everything, objects, information, and "expert opinions." . . . The communication of experience and fantasies was pleasing to the conscience. Collective introspection provided models for putting the self into words. The repertoire of shared knowledge grew.[12]

Ernaux's reminiscences almost always take the form of matter. Throughout the novel, the unspontaneous desire of voluntary reminiscence is dependent upon inscription of memories in material objects and technologies, as if she is indeed examining the phantasmagorias of culture through the examination of its residues. She describes her memories as they are raised from photos, personal diaries, or VHS tapes.[13] *The Years* is therefore not only a novel tracing memory but a book tracing the change in remembrance vis-à-vis the change of material technologies upon which memories are inscribed. For example, Ernaux describes the transference of memory through cultural rituals in the 1950s, affected by the memory of the war: "Memory was transmitted not only through the stories but through the ways of walking, sitting, talking, laughing, eating, hailing someone, grabbing hold of objects."[14] These gestures, corporeal by nature, emphasize the materiality of the body in the process of memory, a body that would be invaded with the advent of digital technologies: "The questions that arose with the appearance of new technologies were canceled out as their use became second nature, and required no thought."[15]

The forms of individual perception in *The Years* thus mix the intimate and autobiographic realm with technical conditions that enable memory for all, so that individual existence is always exposed or involved with the collective through a dependence on obsolescent objects. This movement is evident when Ernaux conceives her femininity while facing women's magazines of the time or remembers her childhood as a "silent film in color," enmeshing the technological medium and "real-life" perception.[16] With the prevalence of private computers, time itself accelerates: "The quick jump-click of the mouse in the screen was the measure of time."[17] The desire to remember is intertwined with the acceleration of obsolete objects and technologies: "We graduated to the DVD player, the digital camera, the MP3 player, ADSL, and the flat screen. We never ceased to upgrade. The failure to do so meant saying yes to aging."[18]

In *The Years*, then, the disposability of objects (MP3s, ADSL, and so on) mirrors the disposability of people. The acceleration of ephemeral technologies renders obsolete not only material objects and technologies but also human beings. This material reflection becomes a reflection on aging: Not to adapt is to allow oneself to grow old. As a literary ragpicker, Ernaux uses voluntary memory to point to a change in the experience of memory and remembrance. She follows the process of her generation becoming obsolete in itself: "People who didn't know how to use a computer or a Discman would become obsolete, like those who couldn't use a phone or washing machine."[19] It is not an exaggeration to claim that Ernaux writes her memoir from the position of the outdated and the left-behind, much like the ragpicker, who lives among residues.

Committed to the literal meaning of its genre as a memoir, *The Years* describes memories while stressing what can be remembered and what cannot, what remains and who is left behind as remainders of the digital era. The process of memory and forgetting is managed primarily by the amnesiac circulation of media: "The media took charge of the process of memory and forgetting. It commemorated everything that could be commemorated.... We belonged to all and none. Our years were nowhere among them."[20] Similar is the abundance of memories inscribed on digital technologies, which are themselves amnesiac: "Our photographs and films—filed by date and viewed onscreen, one after the other without a pause—were pervaded by the light of a time that was unique, no matter how diverse the scenes and landscapes. Another form of past came into being, fluid, with little real memory content."[21] It is Ernaux's mission, voluntary and methodical, to counter this amnesia with her writing, to salvage waste, as well as forgotten beliefs and promises from the collective past, as a literary ragpicker.

This movement is fully realized in Ernaux's later work, *A Girl's Story* (*Mémoire de fille*), in which she revisits a traumatic event from her adolescence. In the summer of 1958, she was raped by a boy at a French summer camp. This event creates a fissure in the author's memory; it produces a gap between her reflective voice in the present and the girl who becomes the object of the writing—the innocent, clueless girl she once was. Throughout the book, this temporal and affective distance is made visible in Ernaux's insistence on referring to her former self periphrastically—as "the girl of '58," "Annie D.," or simply "she":

> That being the case, am I to dissolve the girl of '58 and the woman of 2014 into a single "I"? Or proceed in a way that is, if not the most precise (a subjective

> evaluation), certainly the most adventurous, which is to say, to dissociate the former from the latter through the use of "she" and "I."[22]

The 1958 version of Ernaux becomes obsolete in the sense that she cannot be integrated into a coherent self-narrative. She is observed only through a reflective rupture, as someone irretrievably distant. Ernaux underscores this disconnection through the absence of media: "There are no photos of her from the summer of 1958"; "I see but do not hear her. There exists no recording of my voice of 1958, and the words we ourselves speak are transcribed by memory unvoiced."[23] In this sense, it is not simply the memory that becomes obsolete but the self who experienced it.

This form of impersonal detachment—so central to *The Years*, where it enabled a kind of collective autobiography—reappears here in relation to trauma, bullying, and humiliation. But rather than resulting in silence or disappearance, it becomes the condition for writing. The alienation from the self becomes the very mode through which memory, now estranged and dispassionate, can return. Ernaux insists on remembering the girl of 1958—salvaging her, like a ragpicker, from oblivion. She does this through writing, but in a form of writing that reinserts the real, the tangible, and the material into the immateriality of memory:

> I wanted physical, tangible proof of their existence,
> as if to continue writing I needed them to be alive,
> as if I needed to be writing about what is alive,
> to be endangered in the way one is when writing
> about the living and not in the state of tranquility
> that prevails when people die and are consigned to
> the immateriality of fictional characters. There is
> a need to make writing an untenable enterprise, to
> atone for its power (not its ease, no one feels less ease

in writing than me) out of an imaginary terror of consequences.[24]

This passage illuminates Ernaux's poetics of ragpicking, now turned inward. Writing becomes a form of recovery—not of personal coherence but of contact with what is already obsolete. Ernaux does not become Annie of 1958 by the end of the narrative; rather, her dispossession from that former self—her estranged relation to obsolete versions of herself—is what enables her to approach them as one approaches refuse: with distance, hesitancy, and persistence. It is also what allows her to write from a threshold where memory becomes collective. From this position, she is able to render memory not as redemptive personal confession but as shared residue.

Restroom Deserts

The excerpts from *The Years* position Ernaux in alignment with the practice of ragpicking, in which the writer—like the ragpicker—engages with collective fantasies through the discarded detritus of obsolete commodities. More than this, as *A Girl's Story* also demonstrates, Ernaux's narration adopts an impersonal voice, as if surrendering individual subjectivity to a collective consciousness while lingering on both personal and collective residues. Yet ragpicking is inseparable from its urban context—the stage on which impersonal memory intersects with the anonymity of the city crowd. As a dweller in public urban space, the ragpicker encounters discarded materials from bourgeois households in the cohesive mass of the modern city, making a living from its industrial residues. Ernaux's oeuvre is deeply engaged with urban space, but with its postindustrial formation—a space in which the visibility and circulation of waste have radically changed. To contextualize this shift, I turn briefly to the changing visibility of waste in present-day New York City, placing it in dialogue with Dominique Laporte's critique of urban sanitation and the management of residue.

The HBO documentary series *How To with John Wilson* illustrates how, in New York City, private space is celebrated at the expense of the public commons—the natural terrain of the ragpicker. Each episode centers around a tutorial-like theme, often featuring topics familiar to New Yorkers ("How to Put Up Scaffolding," "How to Find a Spot"), and delves into the everyday nuances of contemporary urban life. Cinematically, Wilson's work mirrors, to some extent, the practice of ragpicking: Alongside his voiceover narration, *How To* assembles footage of seemingly insignificant and discarded moments captured on his camera—scenes of an anonymous New York resident using dental floss, a dog adorned in a puffy jacket, an abandoned teddy bear on an NYC street, or a piece of chewing gum stuck to a trash bin, among others. Through its lens, *How To* reveals the comic yet also unsettlingly bizarre aspects of New York City's public sphere, including moments like a man casually scratching his groin on the subway.

In the *How To* episode exemplifying the theme of waste in the postindustrial city, titled "How to Find a Public Restroom," Wilson encounters the frustrating reality of being denied access to restroom facilities.[25] While restaurants' restrooms are reserved for "paying customers," Wilson showcases the state of New York City's public restrooms, a result of budget cuts in the 1970s. Many of these facilities have deteriorated to the point of being scarcely functional, with some lacking doors, ostensibly to prevent drug use. Recently, the city installed a mere five automatic public restroom booths to serve its five boroughs (Wilson comically finds himself caught in one during a vigorous auto-cleaning cycle). Navigating through the urban restroom desert, particularly the

Upper East Side, Wilson concludes that New York City is a "restroom matrix" not easily hacked.

This does not mean the city is devoid of urine and other residues—quite the opposite. The lack of adequate public toilets leads to the reappearance of repressed waste in various forms. Whether it is taxi drivers discarding urine-filled plastic bottles or shop owners scrubbing urine-stained pavements outside their establishments each morning, Wilson captures these phenomena in his montage. The denial of this basic human need causes waste to resurface in public spaces, while the private realms of the postindustrial city remain detached from its consequences.

The "public restroom deserts" in New York City can be interpreted as a radicalization of a historical shift, echoing themes explored in Dominique Laporte's 1978 book *History of Shit* (*Histoire de la merde*). Laporte, influenced by both Foucauldian and Lacanian perspectives, offers a genealogy of shit (*merde*), tracing societal attitudes toward waste management. He references an order issued by King François I in November 1539, lamenting the filthy streets of Paris and prohibiting

> all emptying or tossing out into the streets and squares of the aforementioned city and its surroundings of refuse, offals, or putrefactions, as well as all waters whatever their nature, and we command you to delay and retain any and all stagnant and sullied waters and urines inside the confines of your homes. We enjoin you to then carry these and promptly empty them into the stream and give them chase with a bucketful of clean water to hasten their course.[26]

For Laporte, this decree signifies a nascent bourgeois logic that detaches the private sphere from the public and frames waste as something to be confined within private spaces. In reference to Cartesian ideology, Laporte connects this shift to the early modern formation of the subject as an autonomous entity, detached from the Other:

> The sixteenth century was hardly an era of well-tended front gardens, of geraniums and leeks gracing doorsteps. And yet, discourse of the period—legal discourse in particular—reflects a concern with disordered promiscuity, and an ideology linking propriety to property had already begun to emerge. Mind your own business, and I will mind mine, says the individual to his neighbour. What happens in my home, in my family, my dirty laundry, and all the rest is no affair of yours. This little heap in front of my door is my business; it is mine to tend. Mine to see to; mine to mind. Thus it was that the politics of waste branded the subject to his body, and prefigured, not so insignificantly perhaps, the Cartesian ideology of the I.[27]

Laporte argues that the politics of waste branded the subject to their body, prefiguring the Cartesian notion of subjecthood. From this point forward, waste—like capital—became a concern of the private sphere. If we adopt a similar Foucauldian lens, this shift does not signify the total eradication of waste from the public sphere; rather, it proliferates, albeit in a denied and disavowed manner. These same conditions relegate the ragpicker to society's margins, scavenging what others discard while subverting the Cartesian distinctions inherent in King François's decree. Yet, the ragpicker, cast as an outcast, also becomes an interpreter of society. By defying these boundaries, they serve as martyrs of the public, capable of digesting what the city is instructed to forget and conceal.

Wilson's work confronts the radicalization of the public-private distinction in postindustrial society by filling its montage with bodily residues, countering the way postindustrial New York City presents itself as a spectacle—a city grasped and understood through its sanitized, perpetually new image. In this spectacle, waste has no place; it is a foul reminder of materiality, a residue that resists consumption. The city-as-spectacle functions as a commodity in its entirety, private and public alike, obscuring its history, its malodorous origins, and, consequently, its ragpickers.

The Metro Ragpicker

In Ernaux's writing of urban space, the intimate and the private are nevertheless entangled with the public. In her "exterior diaries" (*journaux extimes*, as Michel Tournier calls them—fusing the external with the intimate), *Exteriors* (*Journal du dehors*, written between 1985 and 1992) and *Things Seen* (*La vie extérieure*, written between 1993 and 1999), Ernaux seeks to imprint quotidian public moments into writing:

> I felt the urge to transcribe the scenes, words and gestures of unknown people whom one meets once and whom one never sees again; graffiti hastily scribbled on walls and erased; sentences overheard on the radio and news items read in the papers. . . . It is neither reportage nor a study of urban sociology, but an attempt to convey the reality of an epoch—and in particular that acute yet indefinable feeling of modernity associated with the new town—through a series of snapshots reflecting the daily routine of a community.[28]

Ernaux not only wants obsolescent things to be remembered but also people—such as the unhoused—whom bourgeois society has left behind as its residues. Staging herself at the scene of amnesiac postindustrial space, she embraces the position of a ragpicker who sees gold where everybody sees "waste," to prefer the obsolete over the new alluring commodity. To do this, Ernaux reaffirms her account of memory in *The Years* by positing that intimacy is always invaded by collectivity and never really exists independently: "It is other people—anonymous figures glimpsed in the subway or in waiting rooms—who revive our memory and reveal our true selves through the interest, the anger or the shame that they send rippling through us."[29]

In *Exteriors* and *Things Seen*, this experience is many times associated with the métro. In the narrating voice, Ernaux's individuality is overshadowed and enmeshed with the other. When a homeless man on the train asks for money, Ernaux thinks of her son, who has the same name as the itinerant.[30] She also connects her experience as an author to a seemingly negligible encounter with two adolescents: "In the subway car, a boy and a girl argue and stroke each other, alternately, as if they were alone in the world. But they know that's not true: every now and then they stare insolently at the other passengers. My heart sinks. I tell myself that writing is this for me."[31] Likewise, words and idioms expressed by strangers adhere to her personal history.[32] While the interior and exterior enmesh and social categories dissolve, a certain kind of dispossession emerges. A form of dispossession from individuality happens at the métro, when Ernaux admits: "I may also be trying to discover something about myself through them, their attitudes or their conversations."[33]

The mechanism of repurposing enmeshes the intimacy of the interior—the diary—with the exteriority of the métro. Ernaux realizes that she must give up her individuality to be absorbed in the city mass. Yet this is not an artificial collectivity she seeks. In the métro, people do not associate themselves either with the pure "collectivity" (the major "historical" symbols, like the stations' names, are under informal, alienated interpretation) or the pure "individuality" (everyone is on their way to a job, thus social status is suspended) and thus remain devoid of any categorization and appear to the other in their pure singularity. By this token, the sense of collectivity that Ernaux encounters in the métro is anything but the collectivity of national memory and history, which is often being mocked, by, for example, the homeless man who poorly sings the French national anthem spontaneously.[34] It is rather an amalgam of impersonal singularities, of people always being on their way to somewhere, dispossessed of their fixed individual categories.

In the exterior diaries, writing is the mechanism with which negligible moments are repurposed into meaningful encounters. Precisely in diaries, a form associated with the most personal meanings, Ernaux herself feels alienated from her own memory when thinking back on the experiences she has in the métro: "Reading these pages again, it seems to me that I have already forgotten many of the scenes. It seems as if it is not me that wrote them," as she states on the back cover of the French edition of *Things Seen*. Writing is a tool not only to inscribe memories but also to give up their ownership. Hence Ernaux can make them public, as commons in everyone's possession, in a move that intertwines the need for public space with the need for public meaning in the form of an impersonal diary. This move completes the salvaging of postindustrial obsolescent residue—the unhoused and the dwellers of the eradicated public space—to a sustainable form of art that is not grounded upon a bourgeois logic of property.

In the exterior diaries, Ernaux finds vestiges of postindustrial space and brings them back to time. Witnessing an era in which the alluring new is celebrated at the expense of the aged, Ernaux metaphorizes writing as ragpicking—that is to say, she insists on the potential of the discarded to turn into something abiding.

Life in Plastic

The postindustrial city, as Bruce Bégout has recently showed, is aligned with the notion of disposability and recyclability, as it produces ahistorical debris (*gravats*) rather than historical-diminishing ruins.[35] Like the disposable object, its architectural leftovers become neglected and suppressed sites—residues left behind in the hope that it will not linger in the present. Private space, in parallel, is transformed into a sanitized and timeproof shell modeled on Laporte's Cartesian subject: discreetly bounded, seemingly incorruptible, and free of decay.

Disposability, as an episteme encompassing both temporality and materiality, reflects the extension of the private over the public. Private space is free from unwanted remnants, while the wandering homeless and beggars, for example, become residues themselves—something to be disposed of. Nothing epitomizes the shift toward disposability more than the material basis of contemporary ragpicking: plastic. Before returning to Ernaux's engagement with urbanity—this time through the lens of private, interior spaces—I want to theorize the connection between plastic, as the dominant substance of what is now ragpicked, and the logic of the postindustrial city. This theorization will require another brief contextual detour into the ragpickers of New York City.

In Roland Barthes's view, plastic, within postwar consumer culture, embodies an enchanted cultural mythology. In *Mythologies*, Barthes's entry on plastic underscores the alchemical essence of this material, portraying it as "less a thing than the trace of a movement."[36] Unlike steel, wood, or any other natural material, plastic emerges into the world as both content and form simultaneously, easily molded according to its intended use without the necessity of carving or manipulating any natural substance. A quintessential manifestation of consumerist fixation, wherein material enters the world already as a product, plastic assumes a "miraculous" potential for the transformation of nature. Plastic offers much more than democratization; it signifies a rupture in the ontology of the authentic and the artificial, when everything is plastic, or rather, when everything could be plastic: "The hierarchy of substances is abolished: a single one replaces them all."[37] The marvels of plastic, therefore, lie in its capacity to become virtually anything, to the point it substitutes for nature itself.

Rem Koolhaas's examination of the architectural ideologies shaping New York City, spanning from its inception, unveils a parallel mythology. In *Delirious New York: A Retroactive Manifesto for Manhattan*, Koolhaas illustrates how historical circumstances, particularly the establishment of a modern metropolis seemingly "from scratch," transformed Manhattan into a laboratory for architectural phantasmagorias, a "mythical island where the invention and testing of a metropolitan lifestyle and its attendant architecture could be pursued as a collective experiment in which the entire city became a factory of man-made experience, where the real and the natural ceased to exist."[38] This ideology, termed by Koolhaas "Manhattanism," shares its alchemical traits with plastic: It seeks to exist within a world "totally fabricated by man, i.e., to live inside fantasy." This "was so ambitious that to be realized, it could never be openly stated."[39] Long before plastic inundated its streets, New York, as a phantasmagoria, has already anticipated its postindustrial conditions—a manufactured simulation that created its own sense of naturalness.

Koolhaas's analysis compellingly demonstrates how the

fundamental spatial imaginaries shaping the development of Manhattan align with this notion of simulation. The Manhattan grid, with its twelve avenues intersecting 155 streets, served as a meticulously planned framework designed to anticipate, regulate, and preemptively challenge, for commercial interests, the organic development of a city.[40] The construction of skyscrapers, made possible by the invention of the elevator, represents not only a frontier-like venture toward the sky, which distances itself from the filth of the ground floor, but also, as evidenced by structures like the Globe Tower, a series of microcosms where each level is treated as a "virgin site" independent of the others, resulting in a building composed of a stack of individual privacies.[41] The planning of New York City has predicted, in a way, the postindustrial triumph of private space: "Such is collective realm in Manhattan: its scattered episodes can never be more than a series of bloated private enclaves that admit 'houseguests.'"[42]

Both Manhattanism and plastic are human ventures to control organic habitats or materials by transcending their temporalities of decay, but in both cases time inevitably catches up with them. Manhattan, precisely because it was the subject of architectural fantasies, must grapple with the remnants of their failures, exemplified by Coney Island's "Dreamland" transforming into nothing more than a parking lot. The wondrous alchemical creations and unsuccessful temporal manipulations persist ubiquitously—whether in the form of plastic or as architectural white elephants.

The same goes for the plastic phantasmagorias, as we can see in the documentary *Redemption*, which explores the lives of New York's contemporary ragpickers, now known as "canners."[43] In *Redemption*, plastic emerges as a new form of currency. In New York City, much like in other postindustrial metropolises, ragpicking is primarily focused on collecting plastic bottles and cans in exchange for their "bottle refund" value (five cents per bottle). Given the materialization of Barthes's mythology, where everything truly transforms into plastic, ragpickers can assess the value of items based on their bottle-refund worth. Early in the film, we encounter Walter, a seasoned canner in his sixties, as he calculates the value of his coffee at Starbucks (50 cans). Later, he evaluates the worth of a bar of "walnuts and aromatic herbs" dark chocolate displayed in a high-end boutique window at 450 cans and appraises a townhouse for sale seen randomly on the street at 100 million cans.

Walter's calculations mark plastic as the exemplar of capitalization in postindustrial ragpicking. If commodities represent a standardization of objects under a unified currency of exchange, then plastic exemplifies the generalization of ragpicking within the proliferation of a single material. If we embrace Laporte's line of thought, plastic, as a generalization of matter, is parallel to a mechanism that purifies the accursed to enable smooth exchange. In Laporte's *History of Shit*, privatization of excrement is juxtaposed with efforts to standardize the use of the French language during the reign of King François, offering a refined and purified alternative to the ambiguous and somewhat outdated Latin.[44]

Laporte juxtaposes the perceived refinement and perpetual newness of the French language with the decay of old Latin ("muddied voices and their dialects").[45] According to Laporte, the purification of language aligns with emerging bourgeois commerce, as a standardized language facilitates exchange while abstracting it from less savory aspects: greed, injustice, etc. Focusing on plastic, this comparison could be extended to the realm of materiality. Plastic, much like standardized language, is depicted by Barthes as an abstraction—plastic does not imitate but practically replaces traditional materials like wood and steel. Plastic's disposability and adaptability make it perpetually new and devoid of the decay associated with other organic materials. Both plastic and money are hence devoid of "smell," signifying their abstraction from the tangible and their confinement within the realm of purified signs.

Plastic becomes entangled with the logic of the postindustrial city in this division between the private and the public—a radicalization of the protobourgeoisie logic emanating from "a discourse that urges proprietors to become ever richer, while casting a withering eye on the foul odor of their accumulations."[46] Here, ragpicking represents a residual economy that is entirely disregarded. In *Redemption*, a prolonged shot focusing on a ragpicker's backside elucidates why supermarkets keep refund machines hidden from customers' view ("the bags are dirty, some of the people are dirty," explains Susan, a former IBM employee turned canner herself). Even the five-cent refund, upon which *Redemption*'s ragpickers rely for their livelihoods, emerges as a debt stemming from consumption—a mechanism aimed at inducing guilt in individual consumers—a denied residue of private capital circulating within the city while we avert our gaze.

Under the Lights

Even in private junkspaces, Ernaux finds her inspiration. Ernaux's *Look at the Lights, My Love* (*Regarde les lumières mon amour*) is a project of documentation and contemplation on the supermarket, composed of everyday notes that Ernaux had written for a year about a branch of the Auchan supermarket chain in her neighborhood in the Parisian suburb Cergy.[47] Ernaux's mission, explicitly described at the beginning of her work, is to extract the genuine human stories and lives enmeshed under the lights of the supermarket. The choice to write a "supermarket diary" is associated with the author's wish to save the forgotten. Indeed, the postindustrial city is formed of "amnesiac" spaces—its inhabitants are spectators of detached spaces who cannot encapsulate memories or personal meanings. But through her chronicles, which follow any one of her visits to the supermarket, Ernaux insists upon the importance of the most negligible moments to be remembered.

Ernaux wonders about the fact that although supermarkets are an integral everyday part of the French life, they are not inscribed in the cultural memory, as they are assumed to be unworthy of "representation."[48] Rather, Ernaux insists on the importance of supermarkets for her own personal memory: "Yet I realize, looking back in time, that for every period of my life I retain images of big-box superstores, with scenes, meetings, and people."[49] According to Ernaux, the supermarket can indeed become something to remember when transformed from its "junkness" as a junkspace to become a meaningful space subject to the passage of time. This form of repurposing, of insisting upon the supermarket as a memorable place, is achieved primarily in the decision to write about this particular space: "The superstore and supercenter cannot be reduced to their function in terms of home economics, to the 'chore' of grocery shopping. They provoke thought, anchor sensation and emotion in memory. We could definitely write life narratives from the perspective of superstores visited on a regular basis."[50]

The way a ragpicker can salvage postindustrial waste, then, is to bring it back to time to regain its materiality: turning plastic, literally and metaphorically, into a memorable, durational material. Ernaux construes the supermarket quite consciously as a sort of junkspace, since the space itself sometimes seems exterior to time.[51] Her way to regain its materiality happens via a demystification of supermarket language ("Like. Real Life. Auchan"), interpreting its strategies ("here the usual language of seduction, made up of false benevolence and promised happiness, is replaced by the language of explicit threats") and concentrating on seemingly obvious social interventions: In a quite amusing rebellious act, she even tears up her Auchan loyalty card.[52]

Just as plastic standardizes materiality, junkspace standardizes subject positions—particularly that of the marginal figure who interrupts its flow. Yet within this controlled and seemingly frictionless environment lies a potential to redefine solidarity, especially through the minor gestures and presences that persist within its regulated surfaces. The impersonality inherent to Ernaux's work is found in the most obvious nonplace, as if the alluring objects, the language, and the strategies of consumer culture are where one can truly hide. Ernaux finds her interpellation as a client soothing and associates it with anonymity: "I want to stay in my usual role, that of a customer, and not draw attention to my presence," or later: "I have to go down to Level 1 before I can recover my tranquility as an anonymous customer."[53]

In this way, Ernaux paradoxically juxtaposes the position of the consumer with the position of the ragpicker. For a consumer immersed in the amnesiac junkspace, memory cannot be easily established. Memory cannot be created in a place outside of time and of history: "The curious impression that time here does not move but is a constantly cycling present, that there is no History here. Even my memory is mute."[54] However, writing retrieves memory lost in the supermarket, as writing bears the potential to repurpose commercial supermarkets from junkspace to space in which experiences are preserved and contemplated: "Seeing in order to write is to see in a different way. It means to distinguish objects, individuals, and mechanisms, and to give their existence value."[55]

With the city as its ultimate scene, Ernaux's poetics of

chiffonnage restore the past Baudelairean bond of the writer and the ragpicker. This bond, however, takes into account the shifting material conditions of the postindustrial economy: the turn from "junk" to junkspace as the ultimate postindustrial residue and the refuge that is found not in the traditional modern-urban mass of people but under the lights of the supermarket. As a postindustrial incarnation of a ragpicker, writing is used by Ernaux as a mechanism that at times picks and repurposes personal memories into impersonal memories and, at others, repurposes residual amnesiac junkspaces into meaningful intimate moments that are regained, in their own right, through impersonal enmeshment.

Ernaux's literary ragpicking reclaims obsolescence as both a material and temporal category—restoring the frozen nonplace to historical time and unearthing the materiality effaced by sanitized signs. This effort, as Ernaux makes clear, is inseparable from the opening of the self toward an impersonal collectivity—one that enables a form of solidarity and a reclamation of the urban sphere. In the Paris of Ernaux and the New York City of *How To* and *Redemption*, obsolescence marks a liminality that remains unassimilated by codified urban space. The postindustrial city's rejection of the public sphere and its absorption of waste align with the logic of plastic: a material perceived as a miraculous solution to utility, a currency that sanitizes decay. Yet beyond the façade of the perpetually pristine private sphere, ragpicking persists in writing—by reintroducing discarded fragments into the cycle of time and by opening the scene of writing to the obsolete otherness within the self and, through it, to the obsolete residues of urban space.

5
Childish Profanations

Following the success of her 2011 book *The Life-Changing Magic of Tidying Up*—translated into English in 2014—Marie Kondo has become a worldwide phenomenon, and the "decluttering" discourse she introduced into Western popular culture still remains influential. Kondo, a decluttering expert known for her KonMari method, situates the interior of the bourgeois household as the space in which attachments, desires, and old memories accumulate and assume a symptomatic form. With Kondo, encountering the things left behind in clutter entails far more than a technical reorganization of belongings; it becomes a reorganization of the self.

In her book, Kondo interweaves practical advice with psychological and spiritual insights drawing from Shinto traditions. She admits, for example, that "while not exactly a meditative state, there are times when I am cleaning that I can quietly commune with myself. The work of carefully considering each object I own to see whether it sparks joy inside me is like conversing with myself through the medium of my possessions."[1] In Kondo's self-help system, sparking joy designates an object's affective resonance worth preserving, situating one's relation to it firmly in the present. Kondo emphasizes: "We live in the present. No matter how wonderful things used to be, we cannot live in the past. The joy and excitement we feel here and now are more important."[2]

In Kondo's encounters with her customers, as shown in her Netflix series *Tidying Up with Marie Kondo*, a desire for continuous selfhood amid accelerated commodity obsolescence is associated with redeeming accumulated objects. Kondo visits people in transitional life phases—an expecting couple, individuals grieving loss—where decluttering operates as a mourning process. Each episode culminates in cathartic images of the newly decluttered home, symbolizing individual progress. This redemption climaxes in the individuation of possessions from impersonal clutter piles. The KonMari method begins by gathering each possession category into mounds, emphasizing excessive materiality devoid of symbolic justification. Margie, overcoming her husband's loss, must handle each piece in the clothing pile, keeping joy-sparkers while discarding others and thanking them for embodied memories.[3] Whether kept or discarded, every possession now bears sentimental significance.

A parallel unfolds with Mario, whose accumulation of shoes—some never worn—challenges his transition to fatherhood as a childish attachment defying adult logic (fig. 5).[4] Initially closeted, disconnected from use or symbol, Mario's remaining shoes become a living room exhibit, reintroduced into the commodity sign system. In this way, Kondo enacts a resymbolization, recycling clutter back into the commodity spectacle. The mature position, with which the episodes culminate, is reached by means of disposal—a mature consumer knows how to dispose. As Kondo explains:

> By handling each sentimental item and deciding what to discard, you process your past. If you just stow these

> things away in a drawer or cardboard box, before you realize it, your past will become a weight that holds you back and keeps you from living in the here and now. To put your things in order means to put your past in order, too. It's like resetting your life and settling your accounts so that you can take the next step forward.[5]

Margie's and Mario's acts of letting go of obsolete objects reflect a mourning process for a cherished past self. More than just negotiating continuous selfhood, decluttering narratives negotiate the untimeliness of selfhood vis-à-vis commodity obsolescence. In the decluttering narrative, confronting one's past foregrounds the challenge of orienting selfhood amid the accelerated need to perpetually capture the present moment, as if the self imitates the commodity's aspiration for unremitting novelty. The decluttering narrative thus becomes a theoretical transition from immaturity to maturity, perceived as the ability to mourn past selves along with the promises they encapsulated.

For Kondo, it seems that maturity is achieved through the ability to exhaust an obsolete object's symbolic value and complete a process of mourning, even if the object is ultimately discarded. Each item salvaged from clutter and reintegrated into the realm of commodification is effectively "reconsumed." Identity is formed through the resignification and recommodification of these neutralized, hoarded objects—whether by keeping, displaying, or ceremonially discarding them. In the Introduction, we saw how this interplay between mourning and disposal resonates with Freud's conception of mourning in "Mourning and Melancholia," where he distinguishes between pathological and nonpathological mourning in relation to the ego's autonomy.[6] In healthy mourning, object-drives associated with the lost other are displaced onto new objects. In contrast, in pathological melancholia, these drives turn inward, as if the lost object has been incorporated into the self.[7] Melancholia, then, signifies immaturity, marked by a rupture in the ego's autonomy and secure boundaries.

The decluttering narrative, in its essence, intertwines self-autonomy with the work of mourning one's past: Margie and Mario simultaneously release material possessions and outdated versions of themselves in pursuit of self-growth and transformation. The healthy protagonist emerges as someone free from excessive attachment to objects and the past selves they represent. In the decluttering narrative, it is our own past selves that we mourn, driven by a desire to anchor selfhood in the synchronic present. This is why, in the decluttering narrative, melancholia must transform into mourning to allow for future consumption; discarding the old makes room for new commodities that align with Mario's newfound role as a parent or Margie's altered life after her husband's death. Through the therapeutic ritual of transition, in which every object—kept or discarded—gains symbolic significance, Kondo's clients are able to enjoy negotiating their relationship to possessions, integrating them into a broader narrative of selfhood and continuous identity.

Figure 5: Mario, in *Tidying Up with Marie Kondo* (Netflix).

In this chapter, the decluttering narrative serves as a point of departure for examining the widespread association—especially within psychoanalytic discourse—between immaturity and the inability to relinquish attachments to the obsolete object. What these narratives ultimately valorize is not merely the capacity to consume correctly but, more crucially, the capacity to dispose correctly and without attachment. The hoarder's clutter, like childish play, signals an attachment to commodities whose allure has long faded; it becomes a form of profanation that disrupts the fetishistic aura of the commodity, even as it becomes melancholically identified with obsolescence.

By profanation, I refer to the indifference, excessiveness, or playful unseriousness with which the "immature" self engages commodities—an attitude that reveals a certain uneasiness toward their status as self-justifying, desirable signs. Whereas the decluttering narrative restores commodities to their proper place in the symbolic order—returning them to meaning, even when discarding them—profanation exposes the arbitrariness of their adoration from the perspective of the "proper" consumer.

This mode of profanation, which targets the exchange value of the commodity rather than merely its functionality, is central for understanding how the obsolescence of things becomes intertwined with the notion of discarded selves. Indifferent to the commodity's aura as a present, self-legitimating good, the subjects attached to obsolete things are framed as immature, as though their refusal—or inability—to discard their past things is also a refusal to discard their past selves. This entanglement of person and object, normalized through the KonMari method, thus reorients selfhood around the proper management of obsolete attachments.

The Sacred and the Profane

In the first volume of *The Accursed Share* (*La part maudite*), Georges Bataille delves into Aztec sacrificial practices to introduce a fundamental distinction between the sacred and the profane. This differentiation hinges on the attitude toward the object of sacrifice. For Bataille, "Sacrifice restores to the sacred world that which servile use has degraded, rendered profane. Servile use has made a *thing* (an *object*) of that which, in a deep sense, is of the same nature as the *subject*, is in a relation of intimate participation with the subject."[8] Servile use—or the utilitarian use of an object—is embedded within a cosmology that delineates subjects from objects, often associated with the disenchantment of the nonhuman material sphere. The profane realm, for Bataille, is characterized by objects reduced to "inertia" and "lifelessness," devoid of any intimate or enchanted role transcending the subject/object distinction.

The Accursed Share aims to provide a critical history of socioeconomic logic by examining its negations and residues. In the realm of sacrifice, uneconomic expenditure emerges as a negation of the profane world of utility and exchange. The sacrificial act entails a transition of the useful object into the realm of the sacred through displacement: "It is not necessary that the sacrifice actually destroy the animal or plant of which man had to make a *thing* for his use. They must at least be destroyed as things, that is, *insofar as they have become things*."[9] Total destruction is not inherently necessary for this negation; rather, it serves as the most effective means of severing the utilitarian relationship between humans and the sacrificial entity.

For Giorgio Agamben, however, capitalism radically distorts this religious cycle between the sacred and the profane. In his thinking, capitalism introduces the configuration of the commodity, striving for an unprofanable state. Agamben's perspective on the sacred and profane vis-à-vis the material world begins in alignment with Bataille's: While the sacred signifies objects removed from the sphere of use, profanation signifies their return. Agamben's notion of use, distinct from Marxist use value, suggests a common use divorced from individual possession—a use free from ulterior means and a bourgeois logic of ownership. In capitalist consumption, this form of use becomes irrelevant:

> In the commodity, separation inheres in the very form of the object, which splits into use-value and exchange-value and is transformed into an ungraspable fetish. The same is true for everything that is done, produced, or experienced—even the human body, even sexuality, even language. They are now divided from themselves and placed in a separate sphere that no longer defines any substantial division and where all use becomes and remains impossible. This sphere is consumption.[10]

Agamben posits that the tension between the sacred and the profane is absorbed and neutralized within the commodity itself. A commodity cannot be fully profane because it carries a fetishistic quality—an excess that obscures its potential for use in Agamben's sense. On the other hand, the commodity does not fully belong to the realm of the sacred, as its aura remains tied to exchange, preventing a complete removal from practical or economic concerns. Thus, the commodity effectively renders the traditional boundaries between the sacred and the profane irrelevant, besides some dispersed practices, such as play, where children disrupt conventional uses and realms of objects, discovering new possibilities for profane use:

> Children, who play with whatever old thing falls into their hands, make toys out of things that also belong to the spheres of economics, war, law, and other activities

> that we are used to thinking of as serious. All of a sudden, a car, a firearm, or a legal contract becomes a toy … just as the religion that is played with but no longer observed opens the gate to use, so the powers [*potenze*] of economics, law, and politics, deactivated in play, can become the gateways to a new happiness.[11]

Profanation appears as a potential emerging from "immature consumption" or "bad consumption," where obsolete commodities are cluttered rather than disposed of, or consumed without pleasure and spectacle. The same potential to profane a commodity is what distorts its disposability; the same profanation that strips the commodity of its aura is what transcends it beyond the cycle of "new today, obsolete tomorrow."

The differences between Bataille's and Agamben's perspectives reflect the transition from industrial to postindustrial capitalism. Writing in 1949, Bataille still emphasizes use value, framing the sacrificial object as a negation of utility. Agamben, writing later in the twentieth century, recognizes that postindustrial commodities are largely detached from practical function. Collecting, a practice also explored here, displaces objects from the utilitarian realm, emphasizing their symbolic value. However, through the lens of fetishism, collecting has already become paradigmatic of consumption, as every use value is absorbed into symbolic spectacle. The disposable commodity is already both sacred and profane—or neither.

Obsolescence is intricately tied to this paradigm shift. The cycle of new and obsolete commodities, driven by disposability, reflects the *post-festum* nature of consumption: The failure of present commodities to fulfill their promises drives the desire for the next new thing. In a culture of disposability, profanation of a commodity involves stripping away its symbolic fetish rather than merely displacing it from practical use. Similar to a child's play, profanation must negate the symbolic aura surrounding the commodity, not only its functionality.

Sensitive Cuticles

This is precisely the way that clutter functions, as a material form that suspends the aura of the singular commodity in absorbing it into an undifferentiated mass. In the A&E show *Hoarders*, the pathologization of compulsive cluttering intersects with themes of childhood attachment and trauma. One episode features Gail, who works with the show's team to declutter her home, overflowing with revolting garbage.[12] Tensions arise when Gail retrieves a greasy, long-neglected teddy bear from her childhood amid the discarded piles (fig. 6). Overwhelmed, she requests a break, sobbing as she expresses feelings of guilt and remorse. Gail laments how she "let the teddy bear down," admitting that, among all the possessions hoarded in her home, this childhood memento had been utterly disregarded. Later, Gail's daughter speaks to the camera with exasperation, recounting the distressing nature of this moment—that her mother could feel more remorse over failing a stuffed animal than over the impact her hoarding has had on her own family. This poignant scene crystallizes a central theme of the show's therapeutic narrative: Compulsive hoarders remain emotionally arrested, their maturity stunted by an inability to relinquish attachments to objects representing the past.

To understand the rhetoric of this reality-TV therapeutic framing, it is essential to consider how exactly clutter, as a form, holds an insidious potential to profane commodities of their aura. For Marx, commodity fetishism describes the mysterious, intangible excess of the commodity form, which oscillates between use value and exchange value. As he explains in *Capital*, using the example of a wooden table, "As soon as it emerges as a commodity, it changes into a thing which transcends sensuousness."[13] The commodity takes on symbolic exchange value—a surplus on which fetishism fixates. However, as evidenced by the divergence between Bataille and

Agamben's perspectives, disposable consumer culture introduces a transformation in the valuation of objects. When both use value and exchange value are absorbed into the spectacle of the sign, the commodity's short-term aura becomes contingent on presentational immediacy. Manipulating an object's use function, as in collecting, is already part of consumerism. The suspension of fetishism can therefore be found in the hoard, where profanation takes place.

Hoarding denotes the compulsive accumulation of stuff now recognized as a disorder by the American Psychiatric Association. As Nicolás Guagnini argues, hoarding represents the opposite of commodity fetishism, stripping commodities of exchange value, fixating instead on the act of accumulation itself. Guagnini asserts: "If the fetish encodes desire into a ritualized commodity, the hoard decodes the commodity, destroying its specificity."[14] The hoarder does not merely reject the object's use value; their core transgression defies the commodity sign itself.

Clutter is indifferent to both use and exchange value, utility and spectacle. As a form, clutter deactivates the fetish for commodities in the same way that childlike play deactivates a legal contract. Profanation, in this sense, is reserved for children, who cling to objects that have lost their allure in the adult world. People who clutter and hoard show equal sensitivity toward an Apple MacBook and an old dusty stuffed animal. The hoard represents the limit of consumption: If one were to enter a mall and, by some magic, suspend all classifications and symbolizations of goods—their fetishistic and commodity allure—what would remain are meaningless heaps. By exposing the arbitrariness of this sign system, compulsive hoarding interrogates an expenditure already inherent to disposable consumption itself.

Paradoxically, then, in a postindustrial economy, it is not destruction and annihilation but compulsive accumulation—an excess of consumption—that aligns with Bataille's notion of sacrificial expenditure. In *Hoarders*, some episodes highlight the real estate value ostensibly "lost" to hoarding, emphasizing the capital that could have been earned if the space were rented to another. This emphasis underscores the potentiality of the hoard for profanation: Under the loss of specificity within clutter, fetish objects lack aura, and nothing is prioritized. Everything is important precisely because nothing is.

When Guagnini suggests that compulsive hoarding suspends or neutralizes fetishism, he places it outside the realm of subjects and objects. Certainly, like consumption, hoarding is a repetitive act. However, its desire is not fetishistic, as it does not focus on symbolic surplus value. Instead, it does the opposite. The hoarder's inability to dispose of items stems from a recognition of each object's unique, intrinsic quality—the "thingness" beyond its mere "object" status.[15] Gail, for instance, cannot part with her teddy bear just as she cannot part with any other item in her cluttered home. For her, every object has significance, suggesting an intimate connection within an ecology where boundaries between human and nonhuman blur, as illustrated by her daughter's critique of her perceived priorities.

Hoarders tends to pathologize this inclination, framing it as a fault of the immature. This concept has some anchoring in psychoanalysis, where enchantment with the nonhuman world delineates boundaries between child/adult and normal/abnormal. Harold Searles's *The Nonhuman Environment* explored this, drawing precarious lines between pathological and nonpathological relationships with the nonhuman. Searles builds on Freudian ideas from *Beyond the Pleasure Principle* and *Civilization and Its Discontents*, which posit that psychic life begins in an undifferentiated oneness.[16] Freudian thought suggests that the infant exists in a unified state not only with the mother but with the entire nonhuman environment. Ultimately, in *Beyond the Pleasure Principle*, Freud will argue that the death drive emerges from a desire to return to this primordial inorganic state.

While Searles is more nuanced than Freud on this topic, his argument still frames attachment to the nonhuman along an immaturity-maturity spectrum. In childhood, an intimate connection to the nonhuman persists—such as a child's attachment to toys—but maturity entails a degree of independence from this realm. Timing distinguishes pathological from nonpathological: The mature individual can relate to the nonhuman world without perceiving themselves as "one with it."[17] The pathologic individual, by contrast, fails to achieve this separation, remaining fused with the nonhuman environment in a regressive state.

In several cases analyzed by Searles, schizophrenics, defined by unstable ego boundaries, can confuse self and nonhuman environment, clinging to the reassuring nonhuman realm out of anxiety over losing contact with it. For example, when Searles describes a hospitalized schizophrenic patient contemplating a window in a door, one senses "how utterly unable he was to cope with any complexity in his environment, and how desperately important to him was his ability to register the perception of these simple items in his surroundings."[18] Instead of mourning an inaccessible intimacy with the nonhuman, schizophrenics, as Searles shows, try desperately to revive it.

Recently, Rebecca Falkoff has traced the pathologization of hoarding from a series of "object-oriented manias" defined in medical and cultural discourse from the nineteenth century onward, including kleptomania and various "collectomanias."[19] Hoarding, once a rational economic activity in Marx's *Capital*, has become a mental disorder associated with irrational economic behavior, reflecting the pervasiveness of commodification in every aspect of everyday life.[20] For Jane Bennett, the pathologization of hoarding also mirrors a recurring virtue-vice dynamic. Just as nineteenth-century France pathologized vagrancy while celebrating travel abroad, hoarding represents a form of madness aligned with a political economy driven by overconsumption, planned obsolescence, relentless resource extraction, and vast amounts of waste.[21] As consumers, we all generate trash, discarding items to make room for new commodities. The pathology of people who hoard, however, lies not in overconsumption itself but in their refusal to perceive any object as disposable.

Though compulsive hoarding undeniably brings suffering to families and individuals, its pathologization is deeply entwined with what the clutter as a form reflects about consumer society. Compulsive hoarding is unsettling because it mirrors and amplifies a compulsion inherent to postindustrial consumption—the key difference being the hoarder's inability to discard and their indifference to distinctions between new and obsolete. By this token, compulsive hoarding exhibits a sensibility lost in the system of consumption. To borrow Bennett's framing, in their inability to discard anything, "People-who-hoard could be said to inhabit an 'I' that includes in a very intimate way the nonhuman objects of their home-space, as having a 'cuticle' that is highly sensitive to the tones of thingly ingressions and material vibrations."[22] This heightened material sensitivity toward possessions also represents an ecological sensitivity—an inability to simply discard objects rendered obsolete. Falkoff's work suggests that the hoarder may appear "heroic," embodying "quiet dissent" against the harrowing pace of planned obsolescence by refusing to waste.[23] Hoarders cannot relinquish their piles because their very selfhood, beyond anthropocentric framing, has become entangled with the accumulated things surrounding them.

Discussing *Hoarders*, among other examples, Bennett's work emphasizes the dynamic, expressive entanglements between human and nonhuman bodies found within the hoard.[24]

She argues that people who hoard are overly responsive to objects; their "perceptual filter" for materiality is unusually porous.[25] Bennett also highlights that materials characterized by durability and slowness, such as rocks, appeal to individuals featured in *Hoarders*, in stark contrast to the accelerated cycles of use and decay that define everyday relationships with both objects and human beings.[26] This "sensitive cuticle" places hoarders on the pathological side of Searles's definitions. Hoarders remain stuck in an immature, fused relationship with their material possessions, unable to participate in the consumption-disposal cycle that defines adult economic subjectivity. Their failure to separate from nonhuman objects and achieve clear ego boundaries marks a regression to the undifferentiated origins of psychic life—a stage that mature individuals are expected to transcend. Yet this very failure also disrupts capitalist cycles of accumulation and divestment: Hoarding's excessive refusal to let go reflects an ecological ethic that is incompatible with disposable consumerism. Maturity, in this framework, entails the freedom to dispose of a commodity desired yesterday but already rendered obsolete today.

Figure 6: Gail, in *Hoarders* (A&E).

Unborn Subjectivities

While Bennett centers on the porous perceptual boundaries of people who hoard, my focus shifts to the hoard as a site of profanation. In this respect, compulsive hoarding represents just one pathology reflecting the dynamics of presentist consumerism. As commodities become absorbed into symbolic aura, other pathologies emerge that manipulate consumption's symbolic configurations. One such condition is "normotic illness," which Christopher Bollas associates with patients exhibiting an "abnormal" level of conformity and conventionality.[27] The normotic individual meticulously follows social scripts, but to an excessive, rigid degree. They present as "too stable, secure, comfortable" and "disinterested in subjective life."[28] Above all, the normotic fixates on "the thingness of objects, on their material reality, or on 'data' that relate to material phenomena."[29] Lacking a developed inner subjectivity, the normotic's ultimate refuge becomes the supposedly objective realm of material things.

The normotic's relation to objects thus differs from a child's. For the latter, material objects are tools for developing subjective and imaginative traits. For the normotic, however, objects provide reassuring changelessness. Bollas keenly differentiates the normotic's object refuge from nonpathological object use. He locates normotic illness not in object acquisition but in the inability to enjoy acquired objects. Collecting itself isn't pathological—it is the normotic's inability to make a spectacle of their collection that's abnormal. Bollas explains that the normotic

> is possessed of an urge to define contentedness through the acquisition of objects, and he measures human worth by means of collections of acquired objects. But this kind of appropriation is not passionate, unlike, for example, when a person buys a

> boat and cherishes it, working on it during weekends and learning about sailing lore. Material objects are accumulated in a wishless manner. They appear in this person's life as if they were logical outcomes and signatures of his personality.[30]

The normotic is a very bad consumer; they purchase but do not properly consume. The normotic radicalizes consumption to dangerous banality: In flattening consumption's value, they expose its mundanity. In presentist capitalism, the normotic purchases signs within sign systems. Yet they manipulate commodities' symbolic value through stubborn indifference to the symbolic spectacle, refusing to properly celebrate these signs. Again, this unskillful mode of consumption is associated with infantility, as Bollas links the normotic condition to an "unborn" state of subjectivity:

> It is striking how this person seems to be unborn. It is as if the final stages of psychological birth were not achieved, and one is left with a deficiency.... What is lacking is that originating subjectivity which informs our use of the symbolic. The normotic does not see himself other than as an object (ideally smart and spruced up, productive and sociable) among all the objects of the material world. Since he does not perceive himself as a subject, he does not ask to be seen by the Other, nor does he look into the Other. Having no interest in subjective states and seeking material objects as things-in-themselves—for functional rather than symbolic purposes—the normotic has only partly developed the capacity to symbolize the self.[31]

The line between the pathological and nonpathological also manifests linguistically. For Searles, one marker of mature relatedness to the nonhuman is the use of figurative speech, that is, metaphors and analogies "in which a nonhuman creature or inanimate object is endowed with human qualities, or human beings are endowed with nonhuman characteristics."[32] In contrast, a key issue for the schizophrenic is an inability to comprehend metaphor; schizophrenics struggle to distinguish among human beings, animals, and inanimate objects when metaphorized.[33] The schizophrenic "is too prone to mixing all of them up in thinking—too vulnerable to confusing them with one another, even at a literal level."[34]

If the schizophrenic takes language overly literally, the normotic exhibits a parallel inability but in the opposite direction: an incapacity for anything beyond hollow clichés and superficial metaphors. Lacking developed subjectivity, normotics cannot articulate emotions except through stale platitudes. They speak of phenomena as mere "objects in their own right"; quarrels prompt comments like "you people are just being unreasonable."[35] The normotic does not inquire into a phenomenon's underlying meanings yet gestures toward what they assume is the reasonable, common perspective.

The normotic exhibits a contrary subversion of commodity fetishism, following its laws but with utter indifference. Precisely because normotic illness is obsessed with exchange value without being able to derive gratification from it, the normotic strips away the fantasy from the fetish. This makes the repetitive cycle of consumption appear as an awkward, compulsive endeavor—that is, hoarding per se. The normotic consumes and disposes without mourning or excitement, undermining the very fantasy that bolsters the perpetual cycle of fads and immediate obsolescence at the core of fetishistic consumption.

Juxtaposing Bollas's terminology with Searles's, it becomes clear that hoarding and normotic illness embody opposing approaches toward material objects—the former embracing possessions into subjective selfhood, the latter forcing stasis and objectivity onto possessions to stabilize an insecure sense of self. Both, however, enable profanation of commodities, exhibiting an ethic that subverts disposable consumerism. The hoarder keeps what should be disposed, while the normotic disposes without phantasmatic investment, exposing the arbitrariness of obsolescence and disposability logics. In both practices, immaturity looms, as only mature consumption—the ability to desire *and* to dispose—marks a fully developed selfhood.

Babies and Beanies

For Agamben, as we have seen, the child's profanation primarily involves deactivating the fantasies embedded in material things within the adult world. This process enables a new potential in the object, displacing it from its fetishized commodity status. Crucially, it grants the child access to a temporal realm not easily accessible in modernity. Agamben sees the proliferation of games in modern consumer culture as proof that moderns cannot enter "the lost feast" of play and common use. Yet in a consumer society, children can access this lost feast because they perceive "things" where adults see "commodities." Adults, in contrast, remain in melancholic mourning for the use the commodity promised but could never deliver. This *post-festum* temporality is innate to the commodity itself. Consumers in mass society are unhappy, as they consume objects that have "incorporated within themselves their own inability to be used" and thereby cannot be profaned.[36]

The commodity is defined by its internal separation: promising something beyond the premodern common use Agamben celebrates. Consumption therefore both desires use and negates its very possibility. Even etymologically (consumption implies exhaustion), we consume the present moment in a way that can only miss it. Consumption stems from and perpetuates a melancholic structure of perpetual deferral, lacking the acknowledgment of this anticipated failure associated with the melancholic. Use remains barred, suspended, as the commodity form displaces the object into the perpetual future anterior of anticipated completion that never arrives.

Childlike play transcends this temporal cycle. Agamben places the fetish alongside the toy: Both show that things "are not properly anywhere," as they transpose the subject and object into a liminal realm that eludes rigid categorization as either purely objective or subjective.[37] However, when viewed through the lens of commodity fetishism, patterns of consumption reveal an insatiable quest for the reified object itself, a drive opposed to the playful, experimental indulgence in the absence of an object as manifested in play.

In the text "In Playland," published around the same time as Agamben's work on the fetish and melancholia but preceding *Profanations*, play and toys are defined as vehicles for transgressive temporalities. Influenced by Benjamin, Agamben defines toys as "a materialization of the historicity contained in objects, extracting it by means of a particular manipulation."[38] The act of play, of "making-toy" out of an ordinary object, forgets and strips away the conventional contextualization of the material artifact in a way that distills its pure historicity. Unlike a monument, which preserves and displays time through documentary value, or an antique whose worth derives from its quantitative aging, the residue that persists in the toy is historicity as such, devoid of any other invested value.

For Agamben, the toy exists in the dimension suspended between the "once upon a time" and the "no longer."[39] The miniaturization of a car rendered as a child's toy, for instance, neutralizes and displaces the object's original economic, cultural, or documentary functions. Its becoming-toy transports it to the realm of the blunt diachronic fact that the car once existed and was in use, but no longer.

Without delving too deeply into the elaborated text, which goes on to reflect on the definitions of "hot" and "cold" societies, we can still see how play distils historicity out of obsolescence. For Agamben, the sacred ritual, which stands for synchronized, eternal, mythic time, is manipulated through play, which maintains ritual's form but implements it into the diachronic realm of human, historical time—the "no longer" emphasizing this diachronic notion.[40] However, the "no longer" in play is anything but nostalgic. Precisely because play neutralizes the original economic, cultural, or documentary functions of an object, it strips those objects away from a sense of outdatedness. Play engages a diachronic temporality without nostalgia: a glimpse into historicity as such, to echo Benjamin's ideas.

The temporality of immature play serves as a pivotal case study in line with its framing in psychoanalysis. The prominent psychoanalytic alignment of play and repetition stems from Freud's *Beyond the Pleasure Principle*, in which Freud analyzes the fort/da game he came upon his grandson Ernest playing. Ernest repetitively throws an object away while exclaiming "fort!" (gone), only to retrieve it, exclaiming "da!" (there).[41] For Freud, Ernest's repetition manifests a compulsion to reenact a traumatic event, namely, his mother's casual absences and returns. The repetition allows Ernest to gain control over maternal absence by mastering the thrown object's disappearance and reappearance.[42] In "Toys and Play," originally commenting on Karl Gröber's *Children's Toys*, Benjamin nuances Freud's view of children's repetitive play. For Benjamin, children enact a particular repetitive mode, repetition that forgets:

> The child is not satisfied with twice, but wants the same thing again and again, a hundred or even a thousand times. This is not only the way to master frightening fundamental experiences—by deadening one's own response, by arbitrarily conjuring up experiences, or through parody; it also means enjoying one's victories and triumphs over and over again, with total intensity. An adult relieves his heart from its terrors and doubles happiness by turning it into a story. A child creates the entire event anew and starts again right from the beginning.[43]

While the adult accumulates repetition's value, the child in play immerses totally in the perpetual present. Only pure play can repeat itself to exhaustion, exasperating all adults present. Play, like Agamben's "common use" profaning the sacred, serves no ulterior means. It unremittingly erases its own archive—accumulating neither value nor narrative but enlivening each repetitive instance anew. By this token, psychoanalysis accompanies industrial production in defining and creating the lost, inaccessible childhood sphere through commodified toys produced specifically for children. While for Benjamin toys represent attempts to enter play's sphere, play itself defies linear reasoning. Contra the adult perspective assuming the child imitates the world of adults, Benjamin claims play never follows something else: "A child wants to pull something, and so he becomes a horse; he wants to play with sand, and so he turns into a baker; he wants to hide, and so he turns into a robber or a policeman."[44]

Following Michael Powers, we see how the temporality of child play is ante-festum, as no "I" precedes the exploration of identities: The child "becomes" a horse only insofar as they want to "pull something."[45] In contrast, adulthood is perceived as something fixed. According to Powers, "there is no turning back for the adult, no unlearning or erasing of the steps that have already been taken."[46] While commodity fetishism is often entrenched in a possessive subject/object distinction, play deactivates this because it marks an immature flexibility of ego boundaries, a fluidity imbued with intimate interdependence with nonhuman elements. Only a firmly established, mature ego can mourn a supposedly lost idyllic feast.

The child repeats and erases, while the adult repeats and accumulates and therefore is doomed to the cycle of mourning and nostalgia. An apt illustration is the Beanie Babies craze that took over the American toy industry in the 1990s. The phenomenon is reflected in a recent HBO documentary featuring interviews with a group of mothers based in Naperville, Illinois—the origin of the fad involving the stuffed toys manufactured by Ty Inc.[47] Initially just children's playthings, Beanie Babies became a fetishized obsession for adults. At its peak in the late 1990s, the toys were bought and sold by collectors at triple the retail price and seen as investment commodities. They necessitated security measures to protect against robberies, while Ty received over one hundred thousand daily requests from retailers. As the journalist Jonny Hirsch Blackman remarks in the documentary, "It was a really nice thing for a while, until the adults ruined it." Later in the film, she adds that people became afraid to let children play with their Beanie Babies, as it would endanger their market value.

The Beanie Babies fetish transparently exemplified the allure of their symbolic surplus value, which was detached from any intrinsic differences compared to other stuffed animals. Their initial scarcity at small retailers, and parents' desire for their children to possess the coveted toys, fueled the fetishistic aura. Moreover, it followed the fetishistic logic of pursuing an unattainable, complete collection: Each

Beanie was distinct, compelling the obsessive need to "catch 'em all" in an endless craze over Legs the Frog, Squealer the Pig, or the limited Princess Diana bear launched after her tragic death, which still fetches thousands on eBay for avid collectors.

The comparison between the Beanie Babies craze and the cherished stuffed animal of Gail from *Hoarders* illuminates the distinction between the compulsions of commodity fetishism and cluttering. While Beanie Babies maintained a manufactured symbolic aura fueling the obsessive desire to possess them, Gail shows an inexplicable deep sympathy toward a ratty old teddy bear that no family member or viewer could comprehend. The teddy is considered worthless to all but Gail, who would certainly accumulate more possessions, of which she deems none disposable.

Beanie Babies is a feast ruined by adults or, rather, a feast created by adults as already missed and mourned. It marks the infection of repetitive play by the post-festum fetishization of consumption, which introduces into play its foreign dimensions of time, such as prospective future (Beanie Babies as investment) and lost past (the inability to enjoy the Beanie as a toy). Beyond any actual craze over stuffed animals, the fad embodies a desire to rejoin an impossible intrafestum dimension ("we all want that one moment when we feel that maybe this is our special time," says Becky Phillips, another Beanie collector). Precisely because the fetish defies its own possibility of present fulfillment, adulthood can only aspire to and miss a return to the realm of uninhibited childlike play.

The final part of the documentary, in which the grandchildren of Beanie Baby collectors attempt, unsuccessfully, to revive the fad, is somewhat predictable. The Beanies are now utterly obsolete, stored in boxes and nearly impossible to resell. The fetish that once fueled the craze marks a fleeting desire, unfulfillable by definition and always poised to transfer to its next object. What remains is the hoard: a pile of objects divorced from their former fetishistic aura and symbolic value.

In this scene, too, clutter—much like childish play—invites reflection on intimate attachments to obsolete objects, especially in how such attachments define legitimate consumption and delineate what counts as a "mature" or "immature" relationship to things. In the narratives we reflected upon, legitimate selfhood is imagined as bounded, autonomous, and capable of healthy detachment: a self that knows how to dispose of the past and relinquish what no longer serves. Attachments to obsolete objects, by contrast, are framed as signs of dependency and contamination—a failure to maintain proper psychic and material boundaries.

The pile of useless Beanies represents precisely the sort of objects adults are expected to let go of, yet those with "sensitive object cuticles"—the irrational, immature outcasts of disposability and commodification—simply cannot discard them. Acts of profanation—cluttering, normotic consumption, and the temporality of play—open possibilities for encountering the obsolete object outside the logic of reappropriation and exchange. At the same time, they expose the discursive frameworks that define the proper boundaries of the presentist self and the forms of attachment that threaten to contaminate it. The attachments of those who clutter signal a refusal to conform to a culture that valorizes disposability as moral hygiene, where discarding becomes anticipatory, always clearing space for the next cycle of consumption.

6
Aged Unwell

In *On Aging: Revolt and Resignation* (*Über das Altern. Revolte und Resignation*), Jean Améry addresses not only the physical but, equally important, the cultural aspects of becoming older. In an accelerated cycle of new trends and commodities, the postwar era posits the elderly in cultural alienation, finding their way in an "unknown array of signs" just like "an auto driver who was traveling through England for the first time before the traffic signals had been thoroughly coordinated with those on the continent."[1] Améry's gloomy analogy captures the essence of its argument: The elderly do not simply encounter an alienated system of signs that can be readily rejected; they are doomed to navigate their way within this new world:

> The dignity of cultural aging, entirely like that of the social aging in which it is embedded, can in turn only realize itself in the inconsistent revolt of fighting out a contradiction. The new systems exist. The aging must be ready to decipher them every day,

> without hope, on to the end. They cannot abandon their decomposing arrangements of order if they are not to abandon their egos; knowing the sinister necrophilia of their intellectual behavior, they have to preserve a worthless fidelity to those egos. That means: even here, in a hopeless venture of self-transcendence, having both to accept and to refuse their annihilation.[2]

The aged are left with no dignified choices. They can either remain faithful to their own obsolete sign system—adhering to yesterday's fashion with self-respect and a trace of defiance, as Améry suggests—or they can desperately attempt to engage with an unfamiliar culture, only to be exposed and ridiculed as impostors. Cultural aging is always marked by this tragic determinism: "At a certain moment—or better, an uncertain one—appearing from case to case according to a person's particular relationships, each can only become what he or she already is. The chances of transcending oneself culturally are long over with."[3] The culturally aging cannot adapt and ultimately cannot camouflage themselves in the zeitgeist.

The existence of the elderly is filtered through the lens of obsolescence, as they are relegated to detached spheres that emphasize their irrelevance—such as the category of the "third age." This connection is particularly evident when viewed through Zygmunt Bauman's *Wasted Lives: Modernity and Its Outcasts*, which mirrors the logic of disposable consumption In line with Bauman's thesis on "liquid modernity"—a state in which nothing has the time to solidify—previous notions of duration are destabilized. He writes: "Everything is born with a branding of imminent death; everything leaves the production line with a 'use-by date' label attached; constructions do not start unless permissions to demolish (if required) have been issued, and contracts are not signed unless their duration is fixed or their termination allowed depending on the hazards of the future."[4] Bauman's focus, however, remains primarily on human beings rather than on commodities. For him, the "outcasts" of modernity are refugees and marginalized populations in developing countries. In the context of this chapter, the outcasts are the aged themselves.

This is what leads us to the works of Michel Houellebecq, an author for whom the dispossession of aging, white, middle-class men from their sexual and social (but scarcely financial) prime is a central theme. Almost all of Houellebecq's protagonists are middle-aged men struggling with their physical and cultural decline. In his first novel, *Whatever* (*Extension du domaine de la lutte*), Houellebecq situates the current human condition against the logic of disposability, viewing the perception of human bodies and subjectivities in line with the system of value and commodification. According to this thesis, which will haunt Houellebecq's characters throughout the author's oeuvre, the system of sex and sexuality is parallel to the system of the market, with only some having "access" to sex and others remaining in "sexual" poverty.[5] In works such as *Lanzarote* and *Platform* (*Platforme*) the protagonists are aging Western men desperately looking to find their way in this economy, navigating the fantasies of the tourism and sex-work industry. The connections between consumer capitalism, the assumed decline of Western cultures, and the loneliness of the aged are at the center of novels such as *The Possibility of an Island* (*La possibilité d'une île*) and *Serotonin* (*Serotonine*), in which the protagonists are trapped within a post-festum melancholy and facing a world in which true love is no longer possible.

The misogyny associated with Houellebecq's literature is an integral part of the argument. Houellebecq's aging protagonists are true residues of the past insofar as they resist succumbing to the demands of the time. They are direct and obscene, misogynistic and racist, going consciously against the zeitgeist.

In *Serotonin*, when the forty-six-year-old narrator is asked for help by two women in their twenties, he cannot think of anything else but their breasts and bottoms.[6] In *Submission* (*Soumission*), a novel depicting the fictional introduction of an Islamic regime in France, the narrator proudly exhibits his contempt to identities such as "eco-responsible urban professional," the LGBT-friendly club girl, and the "techno-Buddhist," which he aligns with a reduction people to "some kind of consumer demographic."[7] These are, of course, only a few representative examples. If, in modernity, the aged are often exterritorialized to designated institutions—as an obsolete residue of the becoming new—Houellebecq's protagonists are the ones not easily recycled back into the system of signs.

Under these circumstances, and along with the acerbic tone associated with the author, Houellebecq's protagonists are reasonably perceived as already defeated. According to Luis Betty, Houellebecq's characters are caught in a world of "materialist horror," driven by the loss of any sense of transcendence.[8] Ben Jeffery's *Anti-Matter* examined Houellebecq's "depressive realism" from a parallel approach, conceiving the author's literary universe as utterly materialistic, defying any sense or signification beyond the opaque materiality of human existence.[9] Despite that, and in line with the readings of Carole Sweeney and Douglas Morrey, the focus on obsolescence makes Houellebecq appear as inspirited and political.[10] While overtly lamenting a lost sense of transcendence, Houellebecq's materialism is not exclusively led by a pessimistic, defeated vision. This materialistic core—the intrinsic entanglement of the human and the commodity—creates a threshold for subversive readings, shifting attention to forms of excess that exist beyond and against the commodity cycle. In doing so, it fosters molecular acts of resistance, enabling the formation of human and nonhuman intimacies bound by their shared fate of obsolescence.

If the previous chapter explored how discursive forces marginalize uneconomic attachments to obsolete objects, the question now arises: How might these shared intimacies consciously resist—or at least attempt to? The form of rebellion examined in Houellebecq's work lies in the possibility for the aged to reclaim temporality by reclaiming their finitude—that is, by making dying visible beyond the sudden, repressed regime of "death." In this context, Améry's figure becomes particularly relevant. It is no coincidence that *On Aging* (originally published in 1968) was followed by *On Suicide: A Discourse on Voluntary Death* (*Hand an sich legen: Diskurs über den Freitod*, 1976). Confronting the undignified choices that come with old age, Améry interrogates voluntary death against the pathologization imposed by psychological discourse. He illuminates the absurd yet strikingly affirmative dimension of suicide—an act that, even in failure, seeks to impose control over the uncertainty and arbitrariness of death.[11] This is the same Améry who, in 1978, at the age of sixty-five, would take his own life.

In Houellebecq's work, death aligns with the regime of the disposable object, a sudden form of vanishing, while what must be reclaimed is dying as *durée*. In my analysis of his novels *The Map and the Territory* (*La carte et le territoire*) and *Serotonin*, I will examine obsolescence through the eyes of the obsolete—the obscene, the lonely, the grumpy old men dispossessed of the world to which they once belonged while insisting on their right to perform *dying*. In both novels, Houellebecq presents a shared post-festum temporality that binds humans, objects, and consumption under the logic of disposability, where the human itself becomes a commodity to be consumed, discarded, and recycled. Yet within this framework, acts of resistance emerge—entangling humans and objects alike. The aging Houellebecqian characters may relinquish the desire to remain timely and relevant, but they remain determined to leave a searing critique of their era before they disappear from it.

A Matter of Life and Death

The Map and the Territory tells the story of Jed Martin, an artist seeking to survive in the competitive art world. The novel begins with problems with Jed's boiler, which refuses to work as it should, a year after it was ostensibly fixed. The juxtaposition of Jed's timeworn boiler with the seductive marketing language of the different plumbing services ("Plumbing in General offered to 'make plumbing enter the third millennium'") reveals a tension omnipresent in the novel between a material reality and its image.[12] Material obsolescence is posited this way against a circulation of marketing clichés, while decay and obsolescence form the foci of Jed's art. Right from the beginning of his career, Jed was particularly sensitive to the short lifespan of flowers, defining their decay as a grotesque parody of their lively essence.[13] He was equally aware of the lifecycle of other materials he had used in his works:

> From this period Jed had kept his notebooks, which contained all of his drawings. They were all dying gently, unhurriedly (the paper was not of very good quality, nor were the pencils). They might last two or three centuries more: things and beings have a lifespan.[14]

Above all, Jed is interested in obsolete industrial objects. Fascinated by a "prehistoric" camera found in his grandfather's attic, Jed's art studies were dedicated to a meticulous photographic archive of industrial artifacts, from handguns to printer cartridges.[15] As an artist, Jed establishes an intimate connection with matter. He seeks, to reiterate Bill Brown's vocabulary, to capture the *thingness* beyond the object qua commodity. Against any relation of profit or utility, Jed is enchanted by an inarticulable magic he finds in things. However, Jed's naïve fascination with things changes, involuntarily, with his first true steps into the world of art. In order to survive financially, he produces photographs of objects mainly for commercial reasons. Jed's fascination with Michelin route maps, for him the essence of modernity, culminates in an art project in which he is pushed to actively cooperate with Michelin's PR people. Jed's art becomes a pure commodity not only because he actively cooperates with Michelin but also because his art ideally meets the insidious conditions and desires of the market:

> The growing popularity, across all of France, of cookery classes, the recent appearance of local competitions rewarding new creations in charcuterie or cheese making, the massive and inexorable spread of hiking, and even the outing of Jean-Pierre Pernaut combined to bring about this new sociological fact: for the first time in France since Jean-Jacques Rousseau, the countryside had become *trendy* again. Society seemed to suddenly become aware of this, through its major dailies and magazines, in the few weeks which followed Jed's *vernissage*. And the Michelin map, an utterly unnoticed utilitarian object, became in the space of those very weeks the privileged vehicle for initiation into what Libération was to shamelessly call the "magic of the *terroir*."[16]

Jed's art, displaced from an interest in obsolete objects to the terminology of trends and fads, becomes a sign abstracted from material reality. Michelin maps become a sign, a seemingly new and alluring commodity, bolstered by the cultural and economic tendencies of the market, in this case the trendy comeback of countryside gastronomy.

Certainly, in postindustrial capitalism it is not the material "countryside" that comes back as a commodified object, as it is already consumed and lost into its simulacrum. What comes back is the magic of the *terroir*, in the very same sense that the map, according to Jed's exhibition's title, is "more interesting than the territory." This language is under constant deconstruction in *The Map and the Territory*, at times by Houellebecq's ironic use of italics ("magic of the *terroir*") or without them, for example, when fictional excerpts from restaurant guides are embedded into the narrative: "Then you will need only close your eyes to remember the scents of paradise, the fountain murmuring in the white marble Turkish bath which lets one simple truth filter through: 'Here, life is beautiful.'"[17]

Just as importantly, at this stage Jed too becomes a sign with its own surplus value. Along with the success of his Michelin project, Jed begins to speculate about his own value in the art market, estimating the updated value of his works.[18] Years later, embarking upon a project consisting not of objects but of human portraits, Jed will still find happiness in these alluring phases of his career, immersed in the neutralized signs of his wealth and value: "His human relations, already few, would one by one dry up and disappear, and he would be in life like he was at present in the perfectly finished interior of his Audi A6 allroad: peaceful and joyless, completely neutral."[19]

The neutral, peaceful Audi A6 bears the promise of independence from the material realm, the one that is associated with obsolescence, dying, and decay. But soon enough Jed, whose first interests were industrial objects and professions in decline (horse butchers, bar-tabac managers), will regain a desire for the material, a reclaiming of the very possibility of dying. Through lengthy conversations with Michel Houellebecq, who appears as a character in the novel, the entanglement of human and object becomes again utterly clear. First, Jed meets Houellebecq to ask him to write the catalogue for his next exhibition. When they meet, quite eerily, Jed and Houellebecq engage in a conversation about an old radiator.[20] The second time they meet, Jed visits Houellebecq to take his photograph, in order ultimately to draw his portrait as a reward for his writing job. Then, Houellebecq confides in him, in tears, about his transitory happiness as a consumer:

> "My favorite products, after a few years, have disappeared from the shelves, their manufacture has stopped purely and simply—and in the case of my poor Camel Legend parka, no doubt the most beautiful parka ever made, it will have lived for only one season . . ." He slowly began to cry, big tears streaming down his face, and served himself another glass of wine. "It's brutal, you know, it's terribly brutal. While the most insignificant animal species take thousands, sometimes millions of years to disappear, manufactured products are wiped off the surface of the globe in a few days; they're never given a second chance, they can only suffer, powerless, the irresponsible and fascistic diktat of product-line managers who of course know better than anyone else what the customer wants, who claim to capture an expectation of novelty in the consumer, and who in reality just turn his life into one exhausting and desperate quest, an endless wandering between eternally modified product lines."[21]

The author concludes his monologue on a typically acerbic note, claiming that he and his guest are themselves cultural products and are therefore doomed to their expiration date: "We too are products," says Houellebecq to Jed, "cultural products. We too will become obsolete."[22] Indeed, in *The Map and the Territory* the objectification of the thing through commercialization leads to the commodification of the human. To radicalize parallel claims in *Whatever*, it can be argued that here all human interactions, and not only sex, embody the logic of the market. Aligned with the late thinking of Jean Baudrillard, to which we will return, the postindustrial economy is exactly what denies and eliminates death: In the cycle of fashion commodities and fads, objects mark both the despair that nothing lasts and the enjoyment that every form can be recycled back into the system.[23] Divorced from the living material "past," from historical context, the fad commodity is spectral at its core: It is never truly alive and therefore never really dies. Under these conditions, the very meaning of death transforms.

It is with death and dying that the plot culminates. In his new project, ten years after his success with the Michelin exhibition, Jed concentrates not on the objects themselves but on portraits of people. In this current work, Jed shows the same sensitivity to thingness, even when depicting human beings: In Houellebecq's portrait, the author is situated in a composition that centers Jed's fascination with the plasticity of paper and the text blocks inscribed upon it.[24] Nevertheless, whenever Jed tries to find things, he finds objects. The narrative follows Houellebecq's assassination, a part of an attempt to steal the portrait Jed has given him, now worth €900,000. In contrast to Jed's original attraction toward the materiality of death, Houellebecq's death seems anything but "material." Houellebecq is deprived of his death; he cannot become-obsolete, and his portrait continues on living and circulating in the art market until it is ultimately sold to a Hindu businessman. Houellebecq cannot properly die, as he is doomed to live as a commodity, a ghostly presence that lies between life and death that can always be exhibited as new.

With this conclusion, it seems as if cultural aging is no longer the worst thing that can happen to the aged. Even worse is the inability to die. In his last years, Jed returns to work with industrial objects, albeit now using chemical manipulation to accelerate their process of decay:

> He filmed these objects in his cellar, against a neutral gray background destined to disappear after their insertion in videos. In order to accelerate the process of decomposition, he doused them with diluted sulfuric acid, which he bought in carboys—a preparation, he added, usually used for killing weeds. Then he also did a montage, sampling a few photograms separated by long intervals; the result is very different from simple accelerated motion, in that the process of decomposition, instead of being continuous, takes place by levels, by sudden upheavals.[25]

A bit later, we are told that

> subjected to the alternations of rain and sunlight, the photographs crinkled, rotted in places, then decomposed into fragments, and were totally destroyed in the space of a few weeks. More curiously, he acquired toy figurines, schematic representations of human beings, and subjected them to the same process. The figurines were more resilient, and in order to accelerate their decomposition, he again had to use his carboys of acid. He now fed exclusively on liquids, and every evening a nurse came to give him an injection of morphine. But in the morning he felt better, and until his last day he could work for at least two or three hours.[26]

Aging, even dying, Jed reestablishes an intimate connection to matter and decay. The liquidity of his own body corresponds with the plasticity reflected in the decomposing objects he manipulates. Jed does not want to "die" like Houellebecq, to remain a ghost circulating in the market. He accelerates the material obsolescence of his art, to reclaim, even in vain, a state of obsolescence completely outside the cultural economy. Baudrillard's fatalistic notion of the commodity, declaring the total abstraction of both use and exchange value to code and the turning of every cultural activity into a floating sign divorced from its material contextualization, certainly will view any attempt to regain a connection with the material as one doomed to failure. But for Jed, the secret intimacy of humans and objects, of aging and obsolescence, is a final space of refuge.

Uncontrolled Substances

We have seen how in Bauman's *Wasted Lives* the transience of objects in liquid modernity is intertwined with human outcasts left behind. In this contemporary "culture of waste," Bauman argues, graveyards can be compared with museums.[27] Both are enclosed spaces separated from the daily life of business, production and consumption. In liquid modernity, everything dies promptly—but death, and aging as one of its symptoms, is suppressed and exterritorialized. Baudrillard's *Symbolic Exchange and Death* (*L'échange symbolique et la mort*) tackles the same paradox. For Baudrillard, postindustrial culture is associated with the perception of life as an accumulation of capital and of death as the payment due. Unlike the symbolic exchange of "primitive societies," to which Baudrillard turns nostalgically, drawing on Marcel Mauss and George Bataille, death in postindustrial culture does not bear any symbolic presence of its own. Under the bourgeois commodification of life, time becomes an asset to personal accumulation, and death becomes nothing but the absence of this accumulation:

> Value, in particular time as value, is accumulated in the phantasm of death deferred, pending the term of a linear infinity of value.... The accumulation of time imposes the idea of progress, as the

> accumulation of science imposes the idea of truth: in each case, what is accumulated is no longer symbolically exchanged, but becomes an objective dimension. Ultimately, the total objectivity of time, like total accumulation, is the total impossibility of symbolic exchange, that is, death.[28]

Crucial to our context is how Baudrillard situates aging and the exterritorializing of the aged in society within this framework. If death used to be digested inside the cultural and "divided" in a collective manner, postindustrial death is perceived vis-à-vis a general equivalent, namely, value and capital, in front of which everyone is alone: "Everyone finds themselves alone before death, since *death is general equivalence*."[29] This explains how old age has become "a marginal and ultimately asocial slice of life—a ghetto, a reprieve and the slide into death."[30] The soon-to-be dispossessed aged are no longer a part of the accumulating, productive society, and they are left to early social death in the excluded category of the "third age." More than a simply "dead" and "living" dichotomy, the realm of the social, and of consumption, distances itself from death for the sake of survival and accumulation. Death is the one thing that cannot be exchanged and commodified.

Through this lens, Houellebecq's *Serotonin* offers a point of departure for a reading parallel to that of *The Map and the Territory*. At the center of the novel we find a typical Houellebecqian protagonist named Florent-Claude Labrouste. Leaving his job in agronomics, Florent-Claude decides to wander through Europe, and particularly through the changing rural areas of France. Florent-Claude is equipped with enough money to drift between different hotels, but he does so quite aimlessly, without finding any true meaning to his life.

In a fashion similar to that of other novels by the author, namely *The Possibility of an Island*, *Serotonin* establishes a distinction between the past lively years of its protagonist and his present melancholic search to attain happiness to no avail, a search haunted by the shadow of past loves and memories: "I have known happiness, I know what it is, I can speak about it competently, and I also know how it ends, as it usually does."[31] While in *The Possibility of an Island* this opposition is manifested in the gap between the life of a human character and their clone, in *Serotonin* it is manifested in mechanisms of hormones and antidepressants, actualizing the future, post-human universe of *The Possibility of an Island* in present time.

To deal with his depression, Florent-Claude receives a prescription for Captorix, an antidepressant similar to current prevalent SSRI medications. In *Serotonin* (named after the hormone that Captorix, like most antidepressants, regulates), Captorix is associated with a dull, mechanical flow of life. This is similar to the neutralized life associated with the circulation of the human and the commodity in *The Map and the Territory*: a ghostly existence situated between "life" and "death," manifesting a wish to defer death. For Florent-Claude, Captorix also signifies a wish to avoid risks, danger, and the impact of strong feelings. According to him, Captorix

> proved to be surprisingly successful overall, allowing patients to perform afresh the major rituals of a normal life within a developed society (washing, good neighborliness, simple bureaucratic procedures), and unlike previous generations of antidepressants it did not encourage suicidal tendencies or self-harm.[32]

Captorix is also responsible for a loss of libido and exhibits Florent-Claude's inability to relive his past. To attain a true, unbounded form of love, and evidently following a bizarre logic, Florent-Claude tries to murder his ex-girlfriend's son, assuming her loneliness will bring them back together. Nonetheless, when the perfect moment arrives, he finds out he lacks the courage. He is indeed too dull to pull the trigger, and he ultimately collapses in misery:

> I understood that it was over, that I wouldn't shoot, that I wouldn't manage to alter the course of things, that the mechanism of unhappiness was the strongest of all, that I would never regain Camille and that we would both die alone, unhappy and alone, each in our own way.[33]

Florent-Claude is too deep in the spectral realm of Captorix, which is metonymic for the dull, sedated bourgeois life of the postindustrial middle-class man. According to Laurent de Sutter, the sedative effects of SSRI medications are part of a broader mechanism embedded in the logic of postindustrial capitalism. He examines new regimes of psychopolitics in which excitation is systematically regulated and controlled. For de Sutter, every form of capitalism is *narcocapitalism*, in which "excitability is only the manic reverse of the depression it never stops producing, even as it presents itself as its remedy."[34] In this respect, antidepressants function as a form of anesthesia that sustains production and regulates excitation—an affective state that, in the case of political rebellion, could disrupt the cycles of production and consumption.[35] In *Serotonin*, Captorix indeed functions as anesthetic matter. It eases Florent-Claude's suffering by rendering him apathetic and indifferent, compromising his ability to love and to take the risks that love entails. Yet his rebellion complicates a dualistic logic in which the anesthetic effects of SSRIs are simply rejected in favor of an idealized, naturally excitable psyche. Florent-Claude continuously attempts to manage his psyche, albeit unsuccessfully.

In fact, Captorix is not the only substance that Florent-Claude habitually consumes. Florent-Claude's addiction to nicotine is extensively evident in the novel, right from the opening paragraph: "Nicotine is a perfect drug, a simple, hard drug that brings no joy, defined entirely by a lack, and by the cessation of that lack."[36] When at the beginning of the novel Florent-Claude embarks upon his mission to relive his past and commits "social suicide," he is right away doomed to an incessant oscillation between different locations and hotel rooms. Florent-Claude can give up almost everything but his right to smoke inside his room, sometimes even vandalizing the smoke detector so he can.[37] The difficulties Florent-Claude has as a smoker are inextricable from his inability to situate himself in the current era as an aging man, an era in which smoking is conceived as an excessive, unjustified addiction:

> I still had a body, that body had certain needs, and the hardest thing about my flight was to find a hotel in Paris that accepted smokers. It took me a good hundred phone calls, each time enduring the triumphant contempt of the switch-board operator who felt a palpable pleasure in repeating to me, with ill-disguised satisfaction: "No, sir, that's impossible, our establishment is entirely non-smoking, thank you for your call." In the end I spent two whole days on that quest, and it was only at dawn on the third day—when I was seriously considering becoming homeless (a homeless person with seven hundred thousand euros in the bank was unusual, even intriguing)—that I remembered the Mercure hotel in the Marais Poitevin, quite recently still a smoking friendly hotel, and I thought perhaps there was a chance there.[38]

Florent-Claude's body becomes a delicate system oscillating between changing dosages of drugs, from nicotine and caffeine to Captorix. The reader of *Serotonin* is positioned, at times, as a psychiatrist when Florent-Claude enumerates the drugs he takes and their dosage: "The Captorix also helped, that was undeniable, and my daily doses of alcohol remained moderate; it was also comforting to note that I was in a dose of 15mg, slightly below the maximum dosage."[39] The opposition *The Map and The Territory* establishes between the commodity and brute materiality is internalized into Florent-Claude's hormonology, manifesting itself in the distinction between Captorix and nicotine. The story of Florent-Claude follows the process through which some substances are neatly digested into late capitalist culture (Captorix) and others become accursed, defy signification, and present a challenge to this literal and metaphorical digestive system (nicotine, alcohol abuse). In his morose method of revolt, Florent-Claude chooses the latter group. Toward the end of the novel, in a paragraph mirroring its opening, he summarizes this perception of Captorix:

> It's a small white, oval, scored tablet.
>
> It doesn't create or transform; it interprets. It renders fleeting what was definitive; it renders contingent what was ineluctable. It supplies a new interpretation of life—less rich, less artificial, and marked by a certain rigidity. It provides no form of happiness, or even real relief; its action is of a different kind: by transforming life into a sequence of formalities it allows you to fool yourself. On this basis, it helps people to live, or at least to not die—for a certain period of time.[40]

The best way to understand Florent-Claude's hormonal preferences is through the lens of aging and decay. Florent-Claude smokes; he does not "vape." A BBC Radio 4 episode of *21st Century Mythologies* treats the e-cigarette as a Barthesian myth: a gadget that cloaks the stubborn, dirty fact of combustion behind clean, technological allure.[41]

By smoothing away ash and fire, it denies the very material process it seeks to mimic. If vaping turns smoking into a "speaking corpse" in Barthes's sense—a sanitized gesture repeating itself without substance—Florent-Claude insists on an obsolescence that is material rather than spectral, a *jouissance* grounded in actual contact with decay rather than its electronic stand-in.

Nicotine, rather than SSRIs, offers him a certain orientation toward the present. In *After Death*, François J. Bonnet extends de Sutter's logic of anesthesia to its temporal consequences, arguing that the temporal regime of presentism—the constant fixation on "nowness"—is "narcotic" in that it "anaesthetises any anguish we feel about the future that harbours our inevitable demise."[42] The surge of the "now" acts as a manipulative distraction from mortality, aging, and death, possessing an anesthetic force that prevents us from grasping the historical present and its potentialities beyond presentism's synchronic cycle of instants.

This "after-death" psychopolitics is exemplified by the *reboot*—a recycled version of the old appearing as new, dependent on the logic of amnesia and disposability. "Repeat, forget, restart," Bonnet writes. "Such are the three phases of the regime of the hyperpresent, a whirlwind of instants in constant synchronization which redesigns our relation to the real by accelerating it."[43] The reboot presents the past as something that never ages, making the hyperpresent nothing more than the past repeating itself in the guise of the new. All the while, Florent Claude, like *The Map and the Territory*'s Jed, finds his refuge in decay, reclaiming his own finitude precisely when it is becoming harder and harder. In order to escape the hyperpresent temporality (which is, of course, a presentist temporality)—to be able to pull a trigger and break the anesthetic cycle—Florent-Claude must bring himself back to the flow of time, which under the conditions of disposability, which define the old as irrelevant, he can do only through the realm of obsolescence.

This is the reason Florent-Claude ends up abusing Captorix. He takes it in excessive doses and ultimately becomes addicted, having to lie to his doctor to get more.[44] He also gains weight, wasting his savings on extremely expensive food. In his case, addiction is an acceleration of an already established condition. A nicotine addiction, "defined entirely by a lack, and by the cessation of that lack," is emblematic of the impossibility of capturing the present. Florent-Claude is not only estranged from his zeitgeist but from the present and from the illusion of a right and adequate "time" (*zeit*). Every smoker knows that a cigarette fills the lack of the previous one but already creates the lack for the next one. There is no "present" in addiction, which is always defined by past and future; melancholy taints even the most euphoric inhale. In addiction, the present escapes us repeatedly, and we are enslaved by the futile effort to reach it nevertheless.

The melancholic absence of an absolute present, much like Baudelaire's spleen, positions outdatedness against the regime of the timeproof. Florent-Claude does not merely protest the anesthesia of the senses associated with the hyperpresent—an all-too-naïve and, above all, inaccessible realm. Instead, he captures the present by missing it, by failing to reach it, and thus he merges with the flow of time through its melancholic loss. Here, outdatedness emerges as the only refuge for regaining a sense of temporality, precisely because it bears the imprint of time itself.

The subtitle of Améry's book on aging was "Revolt and Resignation." However slight and petty, Florent-Claude's revolt is exhibited by overconsumption, which underlines a refusal to conform to a life that becomes a sequence of formalities. The aging Florent-Claude is alone in his revolt, and the book's cultural atmosphere makes that clear. When his beloved hotel announces a "non-smokers" policy, he feels "at the stage where the aging animal, wounded and aware of being fatally injured, seeks a den in which to end its life."[45] With this gloomy analogy, Florent-Claude places his death in the margins of any economic logic.

Similarly to Jed in *The Map and the Territory*, Florent-Claude is immersed in the production of ultimate waste, that is, unrecyclable and indigestible waste, fighting the logic of commodity's recirculation. Nicotine, "a simple, hard drug that brings no joy, defined entirely by a lack, and by the cessation of that lack," is the perfect example. Going back to Baudrillard's notes on the deferral of death in postindustrial society, we can see how nicotine is nothing other than a contempt toward this deferral. Nicotine cannot be commodified and translated into New Age narratives of self-improvement and spirituality, such as the ones associated nowadays with psychedelic drugs. Nicotine stands for "death" not only because it causes death but because it denotes an absence of meaning in an economy that resurrects and recycles meanings to commodify them once again.

Smokers, as Florent-Claude's navigation between numerous hotels makes evident, are becoming obscene and obsolete, like almost everything else. They produce junk, or surplus, because nothing of their practice can be recycled back into the system of signs. Just like Jed, then, Florent-Claude's resistance is predicated upon reclaiming his finitude, by emphasizing his own process of dying and becoming-obsolete. In this way, both Jed and Florent-Claude refuse to succumb to their zeitgeist. For them, the sphere of obsolescence is regrettable but is nevertheless better than the dull repetition of the new: a never-ending cycle in which nothing really dies.

7

Better to Burn Out Than to Fade Away

"Thank you all from the pit of my burning, nauseous stomach for your letters and concern during the past years. I'm too much of an erratic, moody baby! I don't have the passion anymore, and so remember, it's better to burn out than to fade away," wrote Kurt Cobain—my teenage idol, as he was to many others—in the latter part of his self-lacerating suicide note. The final sentence, borrowed from Neil Young's "Hey Hey, My My," encapsulates a form of fatalistic wisdom often associated with the infamous "27 Club." Cobain, along with musicians like Amy Winehouse and Jim Morrison, died at twenty-seven and remains suspended in the rock fandom consciousness forever young and rebellious. Burning out ensured he would be preserved in his prime.

Yet it is the meaning of *fading away*, as Cobain and Young invoked it, that unfolds throughout this book. Aging rock stars, once idolized, often find themselves condemned to endlessly recycling their past glories in dimly lit venues, with reality-TV appearances as their only fleeting attempts at a comeback. Others descend into obscurity, reemerging only to voice reactionary political opinions online. To fade away is to confront the afterlife of success—not as a lasting legacy but as an obsolete commodity. Fading summer hits, defunct nightclubs, and once-iconic cultural figures all suffer the same fate: severance from the ever-shifting zeitgeist they once helped define. What Cobain seemed to recognize, in the moments before he took his own life, was that obsolescence may be an inevitable consequence of success.

In the cultural imagination, Cobain had to both literally and symbolically die to be reborn as a myth. Burning out is a sacrificial act, a final leap into the realm of the eternal, while fading away represents the slow erosion of cultural relevance. This distinction suggests a corollary: The faded is dated, marked by its era, while the burned-out escapes time altogether. Yet burning out has another dimension. It does not only describe the tragic, self-inflicted demise of an icon but also the fleeting rise and disappearance of the one-hit wonder—a musician who briefly ignites the cultural landscape before vanishing like a disposable commodity. Burning out, then, can signify both permanence and ephemerality. The 27 Club persists as a cultural signifier, still present in popular memory, but inextricably bound to the era that produced it. If Cobain's legacy proves anything, it is that the dated and the timeless are not mutually exclusive. He did not simply burn out like a commodity designed for rapid consumption and disposal; Nirvana is both a product of the Seattle grunge explosion of the 1990s *and* a band that continues to be rediscovered, listened to, and reinterpreted.

This paradox—being both past and present, dated and immortal—also shapes how we experience music on a personal level. Nirvana is conventionally associated with adolescent rebellion, its music seen as part of a phase marked by bedroom posters and neglected homework. This view follows a linear model of taste in which musical preferences are expected to be outgrown and discarded. Yet this narrative fails to account for a more complex relationship with music. In my experience, Nirvana's songs are not just remnants of adolescence but affective conduits that retain their emotional intensity over time. Each heartbreak in adulthood brings me back to these familiar melodies, not as nostalgia but as a rekindling of the raw, unfiltered emotions of youth. This suggests a repetitive rather than linear relationship with music—one in which past and present selves continuously shape and redefine each other.

Music, particularly rock and pop, is deeply entwined with various modalities of repetition. Some forms of repetition—such as aging rock stars attempting to revive their fame—provoke resistance, as the present rejects them as inadequate. Others, like cover versions of forgotten songs, can reintegrate the obsolete into contemporary culture, charging an outdated composition with new meaning. A rock-and-roll chorus repeats itself endlessly, as repetition defines a hit song by its ability to loop indefinitely. From the algorithmic replication of its style to cover songs and one-hit wonders, rock music exemplifies how the present and the obsolete remain in constant negotiation.

Drawing on Gilles Deleuze's philosophy of repetition, this chapter explores obsolescence as a process of reemergence rather than as mere disappearance, reframing the opposition between burning out and fading away. A Deleuzian approach to temporality challenges the assumption that the obsolete—what has faded away—belongs solely to the past. Instead, it highlights its persistent transformations in the present. Through this lens, repetition is not a static imitation of past forms but an affirmation of virtual potentialities that exist alongside their actualized expressions. For Deleuze, repetition is never identical but always involves difference; the past is never entirely sealed off but resurfaces in the present through its virtual traces. Yet repetition's virtual potential is always bound to its actualization, creating an interplay in which what has faded away remains inseparable from what appears timeless. Within this framework, the obsolete and the eternal are not paradoxically linked—they are, in fact, mutually constitutive.

Previous chapters have demonstrated that obsolescence is negotiated through performativity, desire, and the affective attachments of selfhood. Here I extend that discussion by returning to the question of dispossession as an affirmative, productive paradigm. This is the reason I turn to music, a realm in which creation emerges at the intersection of personal, actualized expression and impersonal, virtual continuity. Focusing on different modalities of repetition—with particular attention to Nirvana—I explore how "burning out" is inseparable from "fading away" and how personal and actualized obsolescence becomes the very condition for the emergence of virtual novelty, which escapes the possession of any particular self. Through the lens of Deleuzian thought, I argue that musical innovation depends on its ability to define a present moment precisely by reworking what has faded—reanimating the obsolete into new forms of becoming.

Repetition with Difference

In April 2021, twenty-six years after their final single, "You Know You're Right," a new Nirvana song surfaced. Titled "Drowned in the Sun," the song could not have been written by the long-deceased Kurt Cobain, nor by his bandmates, Dave Grohl and Krist Novoselic.[1] With the exception of the vocals—recorded by the Nirvana tribute band singer Eric Hogan—the track was entirely generated by an AI system trained on thirty Nirvana songs, analyzing melodic and lyrical patterns to produce what appears to be an original composition. The song was released as part of The Lost Tapes of the 27 Club, a campaign aimed at encouraging those struggling with depression to seek help.

The result seamlessly integrates a series of recognizable motifs: the reverberating guitar effects reminiscent of *Nevermind*, the abrupt transitions between verse and chorus characteristic of *Bleach*, and the lyrical echoes of "All Apologies" ("I feel as one").

At first glance, AI-generated compositions adhere to an established logic of repetition. AI detects patterns, and, fundamentally, all music is a reiteration of a finite set of tones and rhythms. The chromatic scale comprises twelve notes, and every popular song is a variation on the multiple ways these notes can be arranged. In pop and rock music, a limited series of chord progressions frequently recurs, often in different orders or rhythms. This explains why the progression C–G–Am–F underpins "Let It Be" by the Beatles, "The Passenger" by Iggy Pop, and "When I Come Around" by Green Day. It also accounts for the complexity of copyright disputes, such as the case in which Killing Joke accused Nirvana's "Come as You Are" of plagiarizing their 1985 song "Eighties."

The AI project implicitly acknowledges a connection between pattern and style—an association long recognized before the advent of generative AI. As Lev Manovich observes, generative AI mimics modern human creativity in its awareness of common structures and patterns from which it attempts to produce novelty.[2] Repetition, then, is not inherently derivative. Nirvana itself is the product of repetition: Cobain's gritty vocals or the heavy distortion in the choruses all constitute stylistic elements repeated across their oeuvre. Yet what distinguishes Nirvana's repetition from AI-generated imitation is that each repetition subtly introduces variation and transformation.

In this respect, “Drowned in the Sun” exemplifies Nirvana’s signature motifs, standing in a metonymic relation to the band’s broader catalog. This metonymy explains why a universally recognized song like “Smells Like Teen Spirit” and a lesser-known song like “Aneurysm” are both unmistakably Nirvana’s. However, despite its structural fidelity to the band’s style, “Drowned in the Sun” cannot truly be mistaken for a new Nirvana song. While it successfully replicates stylistic elements, its repetition is too overt—it remains firmly in the realm of imitation. The lyrics, at a glance, convincingly reproduce Nirvana’s melancholic tone, structured around an enigmatic addressee, a hallmark of Cobain’s writing:

I’ve got my hands right now in every wound
I’ve been here before but not with you
I still got some pain but it’s over now
The sun shines on you but I don’t know how

The unknown addressee recalls songs like “Lounge Act,” “Drain You,” or “Heart-Shaped Box,” while the chorus shifts between apathy and vulnerability, echoing Nirvana’s lyricism throughout:

I don’t care
I feel as one
Drowned in the sun now
I don’t care, I feel as one
I don’t care, I feel as one
Drowned in the sun now
Drowned in the sun
Drowned in the sun
Drowned in the sun

The refrain invokes the same iterative intensity as “Smells Like Teen Spirit,” in which Cobain’s repeated screams of “a denial” accumulate raw emotional force. Similarly, the opening line of the second verse—"I know I'm a weirdo and I like it"—bears some resemblance to lyrics of "Lithium." Yet a critical misstep occurs in the next line: "So in love but yeah, it's a secret." This kind of confession feels strikingly out of place; Cobain's expressions of love were laced with irony or subversion, as in "Aneurysm": "Love you so much, it makes me sick." This "glitch" underscores a broader issue with AI-generated music or with "AI slop" more generally: its inability to grasp the implicit logic governing stylistic choices. While "Drowned in the Sun" effectively mimics Nirvana's tone—blending indifference with sentimentality—it lacks the virtual dimension that true repetition entails. Nirvana would not have simply recycled its own tropes in such an explicit manner, particularly not by borrowing so transparently from "All Apologies." The AI-generated lyrics thus reveal the contours of Nirvana's style without ever producing something that could be mistaken for a genuine Nirvana artifact.

The same principle applies to the composition. The opening riff, echoing "Come as You Are," is almost too Nirvana-esque to be authentically Nirvana. Up until the first chorus, the song's structure—especially its drum transitions—feels surprisingly precise. However, the chorus's final progression seems awkward: Its abrupt chord shifts are too *Bleach* to blend seamlessly with a *Nevermind*-style chorus. The clean, distortion-free ending, evocative of the song "About a Girl," further reveals the AI's methodology—drawing indiscriminately from disparate Nirvana periods rather than anticipating its evolution. Whereas the historic Nirvana would not repeat its own motifs so bluntly, AI flattens stylistic progression, producing an average of Nirvana rather than a singular Nirvana work.

Generative AI mimics brain function by utilizing artificial neural networks that seek patterns in data, much like human cognition. These networks operate on probability, transforming real-world inputs—such as a picture of a bicycle—into model inputs, which are numeric interpretations of the original image.[3] The desired output, whether another image of a bicycle or a text description, depends on predictive algorithms. Generative AI models interpret each pixel in binary terms, enabling them to distinguish between a bicycle and an orange. In music generation, artificial neural networks break sound waves into small fragments, converting them into numerical data.[4]

However, machines do not "understand" a bicycle as a conceptual form; instead, they replicate visual patterns probabilistically, based on previously analyzed data. Systems like ChatGPT rely on pattern prediction. ChatGPT does not inherently comprehend the meaning of individual words; rather, it breaks down words into "tokens" (combinations of several letters) and interprets them as numeric code. Its effectiveness stems from its capacity to learn the various contexts in which each token is associated with others, allowing it to predict the subsequent tokens that are likely to appear in a given context. For better or worse, the power of generative AI derives from repetition.

Here, Deleuze's philosophy of repetition offers a compelling lens. For Deleuze, identity does not precede repetition but is produced through it. Singularities—whether Nirvana, Rembrandt, or Kafka—are constituted by their particular modes of repetition, each iteration introducing difference rather than merely reiterating the same. Nirvana is Nirvana because it repeats its stylistic elements—but never in exactly the same way. Each song is a repetition of Nirvana, yet in every repetition, Nirvana repeats otherwise. This understanding of repetition, we shall see, is intertwined with the Deleuzian view of becoming. Becoming, which constitutes life as a generative force, perceives phenomena as always in the process of becoming other than themselves.[5] Under this framework, repetition cannot be perceived as a repetition of an identity, fixed and unchanged. Rather, identities are byproducts of an unintuitive concept of repetition: a repetition that differs. Nirvana repeats but nevertheless becomes different from itself, repeating and differing via repetition.

Without an assumption of fixed identity, AI should, in theory, be well equipped to disrupt preconceptions of style. Neural networks, after all, do not presuppose an essence of "shoes" or "love" but instead recognize patterns across variations. However, AI fails precisely at the point where Nirvana succeeds: in producing virtual becomings through repetition. AI-generated Nirvana operates within the domain of the *possible*—reproducing existing data—but repetition also unfolds within the *virtual*, introducing transformations that cannot be mechanically anticipated. For Deleuze, the possible is not at all the virtual.[6] The possible is predesignated—it is what could be thought from the position of the present, but it does not introduce novelty that disrupts that already conditioned position. Moreover, the possible has a limited value of duration because it follows an all-or-nothing logic: either something exists or does not exist—burning out or fading away.[7] While the virtual is manifested in actualities, the exhausted form of the possible is realization, that is, the exhaustion of something that is already imagined in the present.

In contrast, the virtual is a potential that is not limited to the real. Deleuze illustrates this understanding of repetition as novelty via the metaphor of learning to swim. One does not master swimming by mimicking a set of fixed movements on land; rather, one must engage with the shifting, unpredictable nature of waves:

> The movement of the swimmer does not resemble that of the wave, in particular, the movements of the

> swimming instructor which we reproduce on the sand bear no relation to the movements of the wave, which we learn to deal with only by grasping the former in practice as signs. . . . We learn nothing from those who say "Do as I do." Our only teachers are those who tell us "do with me," and are able to emit signs to be developed in heterogeneity rather than propose gestures for us to reproduce.[8]

The distinction between reproducing gestures and interpreting "signs," a central concept in Deleuze's work, including his book on Proust, hinges on the contrast between actuality and virtuality. A sign, as we will see further on, is precisely what can be repeated while simultaneously changing and becoming other (in this context, Nirvana, Kafka, and Rembrandt are makers of signs). Since no two waves or bodies are identical, the process of learning must incorporate virtual elements. Rather than merely replicating specific instances or interactions between bodies and waves, we must grasp the potentialities inherent in them—that is, understand how they can transform or adapt in various circumstances:

> When a body combines some of its own distinctive points with those of a wave, it espouses the principle of a repetition which is no longer that of the Same, but involves the Other—involves difference, from one wave and one gesture to another, and carries that difference through the repetitive space thereby constituted. To learn is indeed to constitute this space of an encounter with signs, in which the distinctive points renew themselves in each other, and repetition takes shape while disguising itself.[9]

Similarly, Nirvana is not simply a sum of past stylistic markers but an ongoing negotiation between continuity and transformation. AI, however, is confined to possibilities: It can only reproduce previous Nirvana songs and is incapable of grasping their virtual potential. Thus, AI-generated music, while capable of sophisticated mimicry, remains bound by a paradox: It can replicate patterns but cannot internalize the process by which repetition generates difference. "Drowned in the Sun" repeats Nirvana's past, but it fails to articulate what Nirvana *could become*.

In Praise of the Actual

If the virtual is a potential not always made visible, it is in actuality—at the risk of fading away—that we can sense its productivity. The awkwardness of "Drowned in the Sun" only underscores the need for an interplay between the virtual and the actual—and, I would argue, an inherent bond between perpetual relevancy and obsolescence. The AI-generated song produces an average of Nirvana's style, much like a stock photo unstamped in time: an amalgam of Nirvana's phases that, by striving to be universally "right," becomes utterly wrong. Rather than revisiting the performative nature of asymptotic representation, as we have previously explored in the context of stock photography, I want to draw from this AI experiment a different insight—the fact that true becoming is only possible through the actual: the dated, the stamped, and the irreducibly situated.

The 27 Club AI project employed Google's Magenta program, which, in August 2016, produced the first AI-composed tune. The Google-based researcher Douglas Eck trained the program on 4,500 songs, teaching it to identify musical patterns.[10] Despite this achievement, Eck noted that the AI lacked expressiveness, struggled with musical timing, and could not effectively divide its attention.[11] Magenta made significant progress with the introduction of Performance

RNN, which improved its timing by learning from 1,400 skilled piano performances.[12] This allowed the machine to generate music in fragments as short as ten milliseconds, enhancing its temporal accuracy. Yet while Magenta could now construct musical motifs, its output remained somewhat repetitive. In reducing randomness to maintain coherence, the AI increased predictability, exhausting creative momentum too quickly.[13] The core challenge, then, lies in striking a balance between creativity and structure—producing outputs that are innovative without becoming either too chaotic or overly monotonous.

However, repetition is intrinsic to all creation, and we have seen how the repetitiveness of "Drowned in the Sun" stems not from repetition per se but from its lack of a virtual dimension. In this sense, AI data operates as an uncanny inversion of Bergson's indefinite past, analyzed in the first chapter. As we have seen, this virtual form of memory—one that is not immediately realized—exists alongside perception in the present. The indefinite past preserves memory in an unrealized, latent state, surfacing intuitively when needed in the everyday. AI data functions similarly: It amasses vast reserves of past works, such as Nirvana's entire catalog. However, unlike the indefinite past, AI memory is composed solely of actualized instances. AI gathers only what has already been realized in time, and precisely because of this, it cannot generate something genuinely new. The production of novelty requires not only the actual but also an engagement with the virtual, with music's latent possibilities of becoming. Without this virtual dimension, AI can only generate the possible.

Deleuze's conception of temporality is profoundly influenced by Bergson, particularly in its emphasis on the interplay between actuality and virtuality. In "The Possible and the Real," Bergson describes a question he was asked about the way he imagines "the great dramatic work of the future," a question to which he humbly replies that he cannot answer because such a work "is not yet possible." When his interlocutor insists that the work must be possible—since the conditions for its creation already exist—Bergson responds that the work, at best, "will have been possible."[14] In other words, the possibility of a work's emergence, like the possibility of any true novelty, is not given in advance but only becomes apparent retroactively: "It is the real which makes itself possible, and not the possible which becomes real."[15] A realized potential is what renders potentiality visible, not the other way around.

By provocatively challenging the idea that the possible is lesser than the real, Bergson develops his strongest argument for actuality. Not to be confused with Deleuze's notion of the possible, Bergson's *possible* could refer both to a nonvirtual possibility, possibility as an "absence of hindrance," and to an unforeseen novelty, the potential for radical change. All the while, the *real* refers to what has already been realized and exhausted. Bergson's aim is to show that once novelty is realized, we mistakenly project its prior possibility into the past. We perceive something as possible retroactively, in the context of unforeseeable novelty, only once it was realized.[16] Potentiality does not precede realization but emerges simultaneously with it.

Crucially for our context, Bergson's argument leaves aside systems governed by mathematical laws—such as today's generative AI. For Bergson, in "closed systems," possibility does precede realization, but only because such systems are abstracted from duration.[17] Inert phenomena, when subjected to consciousness, acquire temporal depth, making genuine novelty possible—one that exceeds the predictable possibilities of algorithmic outcomes. This is where the power of actuality asserts itself: If generative AI produces only shallow novelty, it is because novelty is not merely "a re-arrangement of former elements," which aptly describes, in Bergson's own words, a mechanism similar to how "Drowned in the Sun" was created.[18] A potential that exceeds the "re-arrangement of former elements" cannot emerge without an actuality stamped in time, that is, without an actuality always at the risk of becoming obsolete. The virtual does not exclude the actual; rather, the two precondition each other. With this understanding, we can see how the dated and the stamped—what is fading away—does not simply oppose the burned-out but serves as its complementary force.

Blocs of Sensations

Our discussion challenges Cobain's fear of obsolescence, which arises from his perception of rock music history as a linear progression—where potentialities are realized, stamped in their time, and ultimately exhausted forever. In his journal, Cobain writes: "God I'm so sick of Rock Trivia, big deal it's like what am I gonna do when I'm old, if I already know everything about Rock N Roll by the time I'm 19? God only knows that there's no facts to be learned about all these worthless ripoff nostalgic bands of the 80's."[19] Elsewhere, he remarks, "I hope I die before I turn Pete Townsend," clarifying later: "Before hair loss and bad credit."[20] For Cobain, rock history unfolds as a relentless continuum of novelty followed by decline, where potential is exhausted in its prime and, once spent, lingers only as a hollow afterlife and a symbol of despair.

Yet if the actualized and the virtual go hand in hand, we must rethink the opposition between the timeless relevancy of the 27 Club and the decline of phenomena stamped by their time, such as, for Cobain, Pete Townsend and the Who. Repetition, after all, is not a reiteration of something fixed in the past but of something that accommodates difference in the present: It is inseparable from becoming. As Deleuze elaborates in "Literature and Life," literature serves as a vehicle for transcending the boundaries of the subject, enabling experiments in "becoming-other"—whether woman, animal, or child.[21] Rather than merely representing life, literature *is* life, insofar as writing constitutes an experiment with transgressive affects and percepts—a manifestation of the continuous process of becoming that disrupts a fixed perception of the sensing self.[22] In this respect, Proust does not revisit fixed memories from the past but experiments with ever-changing percepts of becoming-child in the present.

This process of becoming is not confined to literature; it is in perpetual motion and merely facilitated by artistic creation. Moreover, this form of becoming is inseparable from repetition. With each actual repetition of a sensation—such as the Proustian child's agonizing wait in bed, anticipating a kiss from his mother—one participates in the becoming-other of this sensation, in its ever-changing interplay of repetition and difference. Similarly, with each repeated audition of Nirvana's "Lithium," "Aneurysm," or "Serve the Servants," I am not simply revisiting a fixed, personal past presumed to be in my possession. Rather, I am engaging in becoming-teenager, an experiment that redefines this actual past within an impersonal realm. In this realm, adolescence does not signify a distant, past selfhood: It goes beyond selfhood itself, negotiating virtual signs in an ongoing process of becoming and changing.

It is the Deleuzian impersonal sign that elucidates how music could be simultaneously dated and ever-relevant in the present. Already for the earlier Deleuzian discussions of Proust, "truth" resided in the impersonal sign created by art.[23] Truth resides in liberating signs from their material existence and from an object/subject position, with Proust's À *la recherche* perceived as a narrative of apprenticeship that culminates in this understanding.[24] In this context, Proust's madeleine is not construed as literary excellence when it reminds Marcel of the Combray that he had experienced individually. Rather, Proust extracts from the madeleine a Combray that neither Marcel nor anybody else has practically experienced; it is Combray in its essence, Combray itself, that Proust ingeniously extracts from the petite madeleine.[25]

Essence, for Deleuze and Guattari, is paradoxically ever-changing. In *What Is Philosophy?* they celebrate this impersonal Combray; Combray "as it never was, is, or will be lived; Combray as cathedral or monument."[26] In Deleuze and Guattari's aesthetic theory, every work of art is a monument, in the sense that it introduces impersonal percepts and sensations divorced from the perception or sensation of an individual. This is why, for them, the monument in this context does not fixate on the past, as in personal memories, but constitutes "a bloc of present sensations that owe their preservation only to themselves."[27] Proust does not write from childhood memories but through a process of becoming-child in the present (a process music is full of, Deleuze and Guattari add). Proust does not depict fixed, personal memories but experiments, in the present, with the virtual sensations of what it means to be a child. Proust, or any repetition of Combray by him or his readers, is at once identifying and transforming what has been thought to be fixed in the past.

What makes À *la recherche* a work of art, therefore, is precisely the fact that Proust cannot own Combray but can only experiment with it: "We attain to the percept and the affect only as to autonomous and sufficient beings that no longer owe anything to those who experience or have experienced them."[28] The redeemed past can never be possessed insofar as it is under constant virtual transformation. This explains the paradoxical ache of each teenager, as Nirvana is simultaneously theirs and everybody else's. It is entrenched with particular teenage memories, as if an intimacy is established in an adolescent room between Cobain and me alone, while as a monument, each actual repetition transforms its virtual presence, causing it to elude any individual possession. For Deleuze and Guattari, the individual possession of memory resides in the actual and the finite; in order to be preserved, independent from the perception of any mortal individual, the memory has to be immaterialized into the realm of the virtual, where it changes but is not confined to the perception of a single being.

By the same token, the premise underlying *The Lost Tapes* confines Cobain's creative output to his individual limitations—the fact that Cobain, as a singular personal entity, perished at the age of twenty-seven and can no longer generate new music. "Drowned in the Sun" alone proves the shortcomings of this assumption, as music constitutes an impersonal realm in which every individual can only ever repeat what is already repeated. As a monument, Nirvana evades obsolescence or fading away, particularly because it is at the risk of fading way, actualized in time and able to be repeated, exploring its virtual potential for change. Nirvana maintains a presence not only through each repetition of its songs but also in the repetition of its style, manifested in recent music influenced by it, such as the work of the American singer-songwriter Ty Segall. Nirvana is being repeated by actualities, subjected to duration, which condition its virtual impersonal transformation accompanying the present, not the past.

Repetition of this kind is embodied by the cover song. In French, *reprise* describes both cover versions and repetition, making it a poignant example of repetition with difference.

Consider my own favorite cover song, the Fall's 1993 cover of Sister Sledge's "Lost in Music." Whereas in the 1960s they functioned primarily as album filler, from the post-punk era onward, covers were often chosen to express "a group's sensibility or make an argument about pop history."[29] In the case of "Lost in Music," Kieran Curran argues that "the argument about pop history implied in the Fall's covers seems to point to the unfair derision of the disco genre."[30] This makes the Fall's cover a work of *chiffonnage*, engaging with the obsolete residues of the music industry to explore their future to transform.

Sister Sledge's original faithfully represents its era, exhibiting disco's quintessential elements: a pronounced treble bassline, melodic piano chords, and an underlying funky guitar. The chorus lyric, "lost in music, caught in a trap," holds a certain irony, as "Lost in Music" seemed destined to be forever trapped in the late 1970s. The Fall's version deviates from this style. The disco beat gives way to rock drumming, the Casio disco melodies replaced by gritty guitar distortion. Mark E. Smith opens with French sentences pronounced with clumsiness, and the original verses are omitted. The Fall's cover irreverently reinterprets the original precisely because it aims to repeat it, thus exploring disco's latent virtual potential for transformation.

Compellingly, one must ask how the Fall's divergence from disco could advocate for that very genre—or rather, comment on disco's undue slip into obsolescence. The Fall tackles the fading away of disco not by reviving disco but by transforming disco into something else, enfolding it into the style of the Fall. Here, one can find a Deleuzian example of learning to swim successfully: With the understanding of how "Lost in Music" can transform, it is neither trapped nor salvaged from the 1970s to become associated with the nineties; the Fall's cover version is an actual experiment in

"Lost in Music" as a sign, which is impersonal and never fixed. The Fall, at the same time, change and transform their own style. From a linear, progressive paradigm fixated on identities, the realized manifestation of Sister Sledge is inevitably doomed to fading into obsolescence with the disco genre. However, adopting an impersonal lens, Sister Sledge, functioning here as a metonymic signifier for the 1970s disco phenomenon, maps the virtual coordinates that would enable the novelty of the Fall's artistic expression.

Dated to 1970s disco yet virtually accompanying the present by mapping and conditioning the potential for its transformation; dated to 1990s grunge yet repeated in the present and, indeed, transforming in the present with every repetition. The lesson imparted by the awkwardness of "Drowned in the Sun" is that music is in a constant state of transformation via repetition. Nirvana, in this light, defines its age (1990s grunge) and, in the virtual realm, transforms with its age, which is never a fixed, personal identity but rather an impersonal, ever-changing sign. As individuals, we can burn out or fade away—but the role Nirvana played in the history of rock music, its own repetition and transformation of patterns and styles, is not truly theirs to possess. No one has to perish in order to survive eternally youthful, as the past always accompanies present creations, and in music, it seems, nothing is ever truly lost.

On Repeat

Right from this book's Introduction we have seen how the power of the obsolete lies in its persistence. Although it fades away, it cannot simply vanish into the past like thrown-away trash. Repetition is the modality that enables the obsolete to survive against all odds. Contrary to the perception of the obsolete as something exhausted and disposed of, repetition allows it to reappear with a difference, proving its capacity to transform and influence the present in unexpected ways. In the context of music, the scandalous power of repetition is best exemplified by the hit: the song that haunts our minds through its uncontrollable recurrence. As Peter Szendy demonstrates, the hit functions like a commodity: With a dream-like force, it repeats in its banality like the stream of consumption, resonating with the *flânerie* in the Parisian arcades.[31]

Yet the hit lingers and survives precisely when it seems impossible for it to repeat. Paradoxically, its very banality affirms its singularity through repetition. This form of repetition differs from that of the recycled commodity, which presents itself manipulatively as new in order to survive. Nor is the repetition marked by visible difference, as in the Fall's cover of "Lost in Music." Instead, the hit—banal, lightweight, and seemingly ephemeral (consider the "summer hits," for example)—repeats uniquely, with difference, precisely when it appears unchanged.

I turn to the hit to emphasize the scandalous persistence of the obsolete in repetition and to insist on the idea of difference that allows this persistence to emerge. To understand this argument, one must recall Søren Kierkegaard's *Repetition*, the text to which Szendy refers. In *Repetition*, the narrator, Constantin Constantius, contrasts repetition with recollection and hope. Recollection, he suggests, is like outgrown clothing—good in the past but no longer fitting—while hope resembles a garment never worn, a promise without assurance.[32] Repetition, by contrast, affirmatively reenacts the past as clothing that perfectly matches the present. For Constantius, repetition is the key to a joyful life:

> He who will only hope is cowardly. He who wants only to recollect is voluptuous. But he who wills

> repetition is a man, and the more emphatically he has endeavored to understand what it means, the deeper he is a human being, the more profound a human being he is.[33]

Here, recollection emerges as a repetition that is too repetitive—a repetition of the already exhausted, like a worn-out item encapsulating the awkwardness of a past self. Repetition, which differs from recollection, necessarily assumes difference. But the distinction Constantius draws between recollection, repetition, and hope fails to account for the fact that, at least through our lens, true repetition comprises all three: a repetition of an actuality (recollection) that introduces difference (repetition) and, in doing so, opens a threshold for future potentialities (hope).

Kierkegaard's influential and enigmatic text resists full summarization within the scope of this chapter. However, in discussing the hit's insatiable capacity for repetition, Szendy builds upon Constantius's premises to deconstruct his conclusions, demonstrating that repetition is, in fact, grounded in recollection: It proves its possibility by emerging precisely where we assume the past cannot return with a difference. In Kierkegaard's text, Constantius travels to Berlin in an attempt to reenact previous experiences but fails to rediscover the joy he seeks. For Szendy, however, this journey confirms that repetition is indeed possible. While in Berlin, Constantius watches a farce at the Königsstädter Theater and reflects on its clichés. The farce is so predictable, he claims, that it stimulates individual interpretation from every spectator. Szendy argues that Constantius's experience captures the same repetitive magic of the hit, its ability to repeat precisely when such repetition seems impossible:

> This is, then, in Constantin's aesthetic experience, the ordeal of farce, which also brings up an

> impossible repetition—a repetition that is possible as impossible. This is the very repetition that hits, which are also sonorous stereotypes, ask us to consider along the lines of that strange structure of theirs in which the cliché, in its interchangeable banality, is *nonetheless unique every time for each one of us*.[34]

The scandalous repetition of the hit is that its banality is exactly what allows it to repeat as unique. This form of repetition resonates with Deleuze's notion of difference in itself: a difference so pure that it is not conceived as a measurable gap between two identities (as, for example, Sister Sledge's version and the Fall's version) but as a difference independent of any identity, existing in itself and for itself. The hit seemingly repeats identically each time, yet each repetition is unique, affirming the power of pure difference. For Deleuze, pure difference is the affirmative threshold for understanding novelty; it propels time forward without relying on fixed identities. This perspective is key to his interpretation of Nietzsche's concept of the eternal return:

> Eternal return cannot mean the return of the Identical because it presupposes a world (that of the will to power) in which all previous identities have been abolished and dissolved. Returning is being, but only the being of becoming. The eternal return does not bring back "the same"; rather, returning constitutes the only Same of that which becomes. Returning is the becoming-identical of becoming itself.[35]

Although seemingly paradoxical, the eternal return of difference affirms both return and change, repetition and becoming. Like Szendy's logic of the hit, the impossibility of difference becomes the most compelling advocate for novelty. Deleuze contends that what appears to be the repetition of the same is merely the illusion of an exhausted past identity. Repetition necessitates becoming; without becoming, we would not sense duration. In order to repeat—in order to perceive repetition—everything must repeat with a difference. Thus, the repetition of the same is not the reiteration of a fixed being but a dynamic process of becoming-the-same. In the seemingly cyclical reappearance of what was, Deleuze discovers the affirmative power of repetition.

This affirmation of difference in repetition is vital for understanding the persistence of the obsolete in the present. As long as something is actualized in duration, its repetition necessarily advocates a discovery of the new. Kierkegaard, adopting a stance reminiscent of Cobain's, distinguishes between a repetitive repetition—the repetition of the obsolete garment or, for Cobain, 1980s retro bands. Yet it is precisely in its utmost repetitiveness that the notion of difference, as an impersonal force of novelty, can be truly grasped. This is neither the repetition of the recycled (the artificial appearance of the old as new) nor the repetition of the possible, both of which are embodied by "Drowned in the Sun." Instead, it is an actual repetition for its own sake—one that carries the grain of becoming. Fading away can thus be seen not as an ultimate failure but as a scandalous survival—a persistence that reintroduces change into the present, again and again, against all odds.

Envoi

Toward Intimate Otherness

This book began with the growing need to attend to obsolescence not merely as a condition of things but as a temporal misfit: the obsolete as a form of abjection, disavowed by the self in its effort to remain coherent and seamless with the present. What do we do with what no longer fits but still remains? In a cultural economy of presentism increasingly governed by disposability, the prevailing response has been one of disavowal: either averting the obsolete or preemptively engineering timeproof forms of cultural production and aesthetic expression. I have argued that this logic governs not only commodities and media but also attachments, attitudes, and self-narration. In such a system, disposability becomes a mode of subjectivity—a temporal structure internalized in the self's relation to time.

The discarded self is sometimes mourned but more often cringed at and overwritten. Its disowning is marked by awkwardness, embarrassment, and unease. However, we have seen how encounters with the obsolete hold the potential to be more than sites of aversion. The obsolete is a felt duration composed of misalignment, proximity, and unresolved attachment in a time governed by the imperative to dispose. These misalignments—formed through temporal rupture—emerged in encounters with the obsolete hoard, the teenage diary, the performative photograph, the ex, or a disco song. Such moments reintroduced duration into the synchrony of the timeproof: the generative AI song, the plastic can, and the stock photograph.

In this conclusion, I want to gesture toward the ethical stakes of living with the obsolete through what I call *intimate otherness*: a structure of proximity to what no longer serves us, no longer coheres with our self-narratives, yet still persists. This is not a radical alterity but a banal estrangement—the awkward closeness of a former self or a cultural artifact that can neither be fully reclaimed nor entirely ignored. This framework does not seek to replace familiar terms for our encounter with the past—melancholia, spectrality, ruination—but to register the limits of their explanatory power in a present defined less by abyssal loss than by abruptly exhausted commodities and commodified attachments: remainders trapped in their own dated actuality.

To illustrate this form of intimate otherness, I turn to Jay Rosenblatt's short film *How Do You Measure a Year?*[1] The twenty-eight-minute documentary is composed of interviews Rosenblatt conducted with his daughter, Ella, on each of her birthdays from age two to eighteen. Each year, she is asked the same set of questions: What do you want to be when you grow up? What is power? What do you think about our relationship? But just as revealing as her answers is her shifting affective posture toward her father and his ritual. At times she is cheerful and affectionate; at others annoyed or visibly impatient.

The repeated setting—same questions, same couch, same camera angle—highlights the swift changes in Ella's personality from year to year. At three, she wants to wear makeup when she grows up. At seven or eight, she wants to be a singer. Later, an animal rights activist. When asked at age eleven what message she would leave for her future self watching the tape, she becomes slightly apologetic about her dorkiness, reassuring herself that her grown-up self will be "much cooler."

Seemingly, Ella's selves are already obsolete—in the sense that each is framed as a fixed moment visually and affectively sealed by the lens. Rosenblatt captures her image each year with photographic precision, sealing her temporality in a way that mimics the logic of the still image, even as the medium is film. While cinema, as Deleuze would argue, could open toward the virtual, *How Do You Measure a Year?* is composed of snapshot-like moments: a collection of Ellas distinct but sequentially arrayed.

In doing so, the film crystallizes the becoming-obsolete of the self. There is the melancholic, self-absorbed Ella at fourteen, whose teenage gloom seems to betray the exuberant three-year-old excited to grow up just to wear makeup. Each birthday sequence marks an interplay of debt and betrayal: the child amassing memories for a future that will find them unusable. The adult Ella will likely not care about being cool in the way her eleven-year-old self once did. Selves and memories are doomed to obsolescence, with only a few elements—Ella's expressive face, her desire to sing, her singing voice—remaining relatively unchanged.

The film's central question—*How do you measure a year?*—is voiced by Ella herself, as she sings a line from the Broadway musical *Rent*. And indeed, a year is measured—not through continuity but through rupture. We do not follow Ella's life across the seasons, her experiences at school, or her evolving relationship with her father. We know these only through brief references, if at all. She rarely addresses events outside the frame. The year is not chronicled through narrative progression but through breaks—through the misalignments and discontinuities between successive selves. A year is measured through the friction between what she was and what she can no longer claim to be.

Attending to what we leave behind has become an urgent task in a culture of disposability and ecological crisis. One necessary step is learning to face our own discarded attachments. Whether in *The Mortified Podcast* or in Ernaux's revisitation of her past, these encounters with the discarded self reveal more than personal reckoning—they stage a dispossession that opens the self outward, recalibrating it to accommodate otherness at large.

If we ask, then, what are we to do with our obsolete selves—with our outdated attachments, discarded stuff, expired moods? One answer lies in the ritual Rosenblatt creates and transmits through film. Ella's past selves do not return to reassure her. They are also not simply archived, for the archive tends to serve the present's imperative. Instead, they disrupt the present—through Ella's irritation, her offhand mentions of conflict, her cringeworthy phrases. "I just . . . want to live," she says, echoing the clichés of adolescent aspiration and popular scripts of happiness.

We, too, are drawn into this uneasy encounter: We feel the same discomfort, we laugh, we cringe, we remember saying things not so different. We are no longer those versions of ourselves but not fully other to them either. Our reactions—whether amusement, shame, or awkwardness—become a way of witnessing the tension between disavowal and recognition, and perhaps they even become a form of solidarity grounded not in affinity but in mutual estrangement. It is in this sense that obsolete selves and residual attachments become thresholds for a collective experience. They connect us not through mastery or identification but through what we can no longer claim. What we have left behind may bind us more intimately than what we still possess, as it enables a dispossession of the aspiration to a coherent self—one now available to join with other fragments. Insisting on the encounter with the obsolete—as Rosenblatt does with Ella—can kindle a form of intimacy through disownment: a reclamation of time that opens the possibility for new ways of relating.

Ritualized encounters with the obsolete are not confined to the private sphere. Consider the proliferation of "rewatch" culture—particularly the renewed engagement with the early 2010s HBO series *Girls*, as explored in the March 2023 *New York Times* article "Why Are So Many People Rewatching *Girls*?"[2] A striking example is the podcast *Girls Rewatch*, hosted by Amelia Ritthaler and Evan Lazarus. Beginning in 2023—eleven years after the show's debut and only six years after it ended—the podcast dissects each episode with fresh eyes.[3]

The effect is strangely intimate: So little time has passed, yet each discussion revolves around how much has changed—culturally, politically, technologically. Ritthaler and Lazarus marvel that Hannah navigates the Q train without Google Maps and laugh at how Facebook is still framed as "cool." They imagine, half-jokingly, that the aging Jessa—who mocked Facebook's coolness in the show—might now be buying or selling antiques in a Facebook group.

Rewatching becomes a ritual in its own right. It creates a space to pause and reflect amid the accelerations of novelty and synchronized consumption. Ritthaler and Lazarus's project—culminating in their 2025 interview with Lena Dunham—is not just another "Kids React" format. It does not seek the sensational or the cringe for cringe's sake. Instead, it dwells with the obsolete: tracing its ruptures, acknowledging its awkwardness, and resisting the urge to redeem or erase its strangeness. When Dunham joins the podcast, she expresses compassion for her twenty-year-old self who created *Girls*, noting, strikingly, that she used to feel more empathy toward serial killers than toward the self-loathing younger version of herself.

These ritualized returns are not about recycling the past into the present, nor are they about ironic detachment. They mark an effort to engage with residue—cultural or personal—without needing to resolve it. In such encounters, intimate otherness and the gasp of duration become inseparable. Precisely in the fissure of present-tense fantasy, a space opens toward an otherness that unsettles the boundaries of selfhood from within and without.

This book, now finalized, is itself at risk of becoming obsolete—like the texts by Fukuyama and London with which it began. One might read these very lines with the same cringing discomfort that online influencers express when revisiting their old posts. And yet, my only hope—amid the inevitable self-awkwardness I do not deny—is to encounter my past self with compassion. I may not be identical with the self who wrote these concluding words, but I can linger with it—like one might when encountering an old, faintly eerie, distant friend.

Acknowledgments

This book is the culmination of several years of thought, writing, and exchanging ideas with colleagues, students, and friends. I am deeply grateful to Didi Atsmon, Eran Dorfman, Rebecca Falkoff, Patrick ffrench, Hannah Freed-Thall, Netta Green, Christian P. Haines, Allan Hepburn, Tamar Herzig, Carola Hilfrich, Sontje Liebner, Maya Raanan, Marie Schröer, and Sarah Wasserman for their insights. I also wish to thank the students who participated in my courses on nostalgia, the cultural theory of waste, and posthumanism at the University of Potsdam, Tel Aviv University, and the Bezalel Academy of Arts and Design.

My research during these years was enabled by the generous support of a Fulbright Fellowship and, later, of the Minerva Stiftung, which made possible extended stays at New York University and the University of Potsdam, respectively. I am also thankful to Fordham University Press, and especially to Thomas Lay, for accompanying and supporting this book from its earliest stages to publication.

I would like to acknowledge the kind permission to reproduce revised portions of previously published work. Chapter 4 is based on an article that appeared in *SubStance* 52, no. 2 (March 2023): 21–37. Copyright © 2023 Johns Hopkins University Press and *SubStance* Journal, Inc. Chapter 6 draws on an article published in *French Forum* 46, no. 1 (Spring 2021): 53–68. Copyright © 2021 University of Pennsylvania Press.

This book was written during a time of war and destruction. Victims on all sides were in my mind throughout its writing. I dedicate it to Noya Dann, a twelve-year-old Harry Potter fan who was killed with her grandmother in Nir Oz on October 7, 2023.

Notes

Introduction

1. "Kids React To 2000s Hip Hop Legend Missy Elliott (Work It, Get Ur Freak On, Lose Control)," YouTube video, 11:12, posted by REACT, June 25, 2019, https://www.youtube.com/watch?v=8kJyRG1hAhE; "Kids React to Fax Machines," YouTube video, 5:06, posted by REACT, September 17, 2021, https://www.youtube.com/watch?v=9P7hGBoi4Vo.

2. Theodor Adorno, *Minima Moralia: Reflections from Damaged Life* (Verso, 2005), 93.

3. Adorno, *Minima Moralia*, 93.

4. François Hartog, *Regimes of Historicity: Presentism and Experiences of Time*, trans. Saskia Brown (Columbia University Press, 2015), xvi–xix.

5. "Kids & Teens React To Kids React To Donald Trump (4 Years Later)," YouTube video, approx. 6:00, posted by REACT, October 28, 2020, https://www.youtube.com/watch?v=yTYyJTTIXEY.

6. "My Old Content Was So CRINGE . . . ," YouTube video, posted by Kallmekris, June 2025, https://www.youtube.com/watch?v=eCcsnGoAmzM.

7. "REACTING TO MY OLD VIDEOS *cringe*," YouTube video, posted by Emma Chamberlain, February 9, 2020, https://www.youtube.com/watch?v=McYEPIuz-sI.

8. *Vocabulary.com*, s.v. "obsolete," https://www.vocabulary.com/dictionary/obsolete.

9. Babette B. Tischleder and Sarah Wasserman, eds., *Cultures of Obsolescence: History, Materiality, and the Digital Age* (Palgrave Macmillan, 2015), 2.

10. In this respect, the obsolete is closely related to the outdated, which itself resonates with the outmoded or the "unfashionable." I often use "outdatedness" to describe the affects attached to the obsolete, while "obsolescence" remains the preferred term in this book to describe particular cultural phenomena marked by a *no longer*. This distinction stems from the obsolete's deeper entanglement with history: While the outdated object, though out of fashion, is still visible in the present, the obsolete has been denied, subjected to the verdict of history, and—crucially—replaced by something new.

11. Grafton Tanner, *Foreverism* (Polity, 2023).

12. Kate Eichhorn, *The End of Forgetting: Growing Up with Social Media* (Harvard University Press, 2019).

13. Melissa Dahl, *Cringeworthy: A Theory of Awkwardness* (Portfolio, 2018), 8.

14. Bernard London, *Ending the Depression Through Planned Obsolescence* (Prabhat Prakshan, 2024), 4.

15. London, *Ending the Depression*, 5.

16. Francis Fukuyama, *The End of History and the Last Man* (The Free Press, 1992), xi.

17. Jacques Derrida, *Specters of Marx: The State of the Debt, the Work of Mourning, and the New International*, trans. Peggy Kamuf (Routledge, 1994), 78.

18. Walter Benjamin, "Paris, the Capital of the Nineteenth Century [1935]," in *The Arcades Project*, trans. Howard Eiland and Kevin McLaughlin (Harvard University Press, 1999), 3–13.

19. See Lance Winn, "Passages: From Arcade to Virtual Arcadia," in *Shopping: Material Culture Perspectives*, ed. Deborah C. Andrews (University of Delaware Press, 2016), 79.

20. Hartog, *Regimes of Historicity*, xix.

21. Anna Kornbluh, *Immediacy: Or, the Style of Too Late Capitalism* (Verso, 2024).

22. Giles Slade, *Made to Break: Technology and Obsolescence in America* (Harvard University Press, 2007), 13.

23. Slade, *Made to Break*, 24.

24. Gay Hawkins, "Plastic and Presentism: The Time of Disposability," *Journal of Contemporary Archaeology (Online)* 5, no. 1 (2018): 91–102.

25. Hawkins, "Plastic and Presentism," 92.

26. Walter Benjamin, "Theses on the Philosophy of History," in *Illuminations*, trans. Harry Zohn (Schocken, 1968), 257–58.

27. Michael Thompson, *Rubbish Theory: The Creation and Destruction of Value* (Pluto, 2017), 4.

28. Günther Anders, *Die Antiquiertheit des Menschen*, bd. II: *Über die Zerstörung des Lebens im Zeitalter der dritten industriellen Revolution* (C. H. Beck, 1980), 3–45.

29. Anders, *Die Antiquiertheit des Menschen*, 298.

30. See Walter Benjamin, "The Work of Art in the Age of Mechanical Reproduction," in *Illuminations*, trans. Harry Zohn (Schocken, 1968), 217–51.

31. In the original: "Paris change! mais rien dans ma mélancolie/N'a bougé! palais neufs, échafaudages, blocs,/Vieux faubourgs, tout pour moi devient allégorie,/Et mes chers souvenirs sont plus lourds que des rocs." The original is cited along the English translation in Charles Baudelaire, *The Flowers of Evil*, trans. James McGowan (Oxford University Press, 1993), 174–77.

32. Marshall Berman, *All That Is Solid Melts Into Air: The Experience of Modernity* (Verso, 1983), 15.

33. Svetlana Boym, *The Future of Nostalgia* (Basic Books, 2008), 3–18.

34. Gerhard Richter, *Afterness: Figures of Following in Modern Thought and Aesthetics* (Columbia University Press, 2011), 1–25.

35. Charles Baudelaire, "The Painter of Modern Life," in *The Painter of Modern Life and Other Essays*, trans. Jonathan Mayne (Phaidon, 1965), 1–40, 13.

36. Baudelaire, *The Painter of Modern Life*, 14.

37. Baudelaire, *The Painter of Modern Life*, 3.

38. Baudelaire, *The Flowers of Evil*, 188.

39. Susan Stewart, *On Longing: Narratives of the Miniature, the Gigantic, the Souvenir, the Collection* (Duke University Press, 1993), 151.

40. Sigmund Freud, "Mourning and Melancholia," in *The Standard Edition of the Complete Psychological Works of Sigmund Freud*, trans. James Strachey (Hogarth, 1953–1974), 14:243–58.

41. Julia Kristeva, *Powers of Horror: An Essay on Abjection*, trans. Leon S. Roudiez (Columbia University Press, 1982), 2–3; Sara Ahmed, *The Cultural Politics of Emotion* (Edinburgh University Press, 2004), 104.

42. Bill Brown, "The Obsolescence of the Human," in *Cultures of Obsolescence: History, Materiality, and the Digital Age*, ed. Babette B. Tischleder and Sarah Wasserman (Palgrave Macmillan, 2015), 19–40, 23.

43. Bill Brown, *Other Things* (University of Chicago Press, 2020), 5.

44. Maurizia Boscagli, *Stuff Theory: Everyday Objects, Radical Materialism* (Bloomsbury, 2014), 2, 6.

45. See again Tischleder and Wasserman, *Cultures of Obsolescence*; also Sarah Wasserman, *The Death of Things: Ephemera and the American Novel* (University of Minnesota Press, 2020); Rebecca R. Falkoff, *Possessed: A Cultural History of Hoarding* (Cornell University Press, 2021).

46. Francesco Orlando, *Obsolete Objects in the Literary Imagination: Ruins, Relics, Rarities, Rubbish, Uninhabited Places, and Hidden Treasures* (Yale University Press, 2008).

47. See Tischleder and Wasserman, *Cultures of Obsolescence*.

1. This Moment Is Going to Be a Memory

1. Eric Koenig, *The Dictionary of Obscure Sorrows* (Simon & Schuster, 2021), 196.

2. Koenig, *The Dictionary of Obscure Sorrows*, 196.

3. Koenig, *The Dictionary of Obscure Sorrows*, 197.
4. Koenig, *The Dictionary of Obscure Sorrows*, 196.
5. François Hartog, *Regimes of Historicity: Presentism and Experiences of Time*, trans. Saskia Brown (Columbia University Press, 2015), 114.
6. Marcel Proust, *In Search of Lost Time: Swann's Way*, trans. C. K. Scott Moncrieff and Terence Kilmartin, rev. D. J. Enright (Modern Library, 2003), 64.
7. Proust, *Swann's Way*, 60. Italics in the original.
8. Marcel Proust, *In Search of Lost Time: Time Regained*, trans. Andreas Mayor and Terence Kilmartin (Modern Library, 2003), 262.
9. Walter Benjamin, "On Some Motifs in Baudelaire," in *Illuminations*, trans. Harry Zohn (Jonathan Cape, 1968), 188.
10. On Benjamin and anesthesia, see Susan Buck-Morss, "Aesthetics and Anaesthetics: Walter Benjamin's Artwork Essay Reconsidered," *October* 62 (1992): 3–41.
11. Henri Bergson, *Matter and Memory*, trans. Nancy Margaret Paul and W. Scott Palmer (George Allen & Unwin, Humanities Press), 179; Henri Bergson, "Memory of the Present and False Recognition," in *Key Writings*, ed. Keith Ansell Pearson and John Ó Maoilearca (Bloomsbury, 2002), 167–92.
12. Bergson, "Memory of the Present," 183.
13. Bergson, *Matter and Memory*, 129.
14. Bergson, "Memory of the Present," 186.
15. Patrick Modiano, *The Black Notebook*, trans. Mark Polizzotti (Mariner, 2016), 1.
16. Modiano, *The Black Notebook*, 1.
17. Modiano, *The Black Notebook*, 9.
18. Modiano, *The Black Notebook*, 26.
19. Modiano, *The Black Notebook*, 24.
20. Modiano, *The Black Notebook*, 24.
21. Modiano, *The Black Notebook*, 77.
22. Modiano, *The Black Notebook*, 20.
23. Jacques Derrida, "Limited Inc a b c," in *Limited Inc*, trans. Samuel Weber (Northwestern University Press, 1988), 47–50.

24. Modiano, *The Black Notebook*, 20.

25. Modiano, *The Black Notebook*, 38.

26. Modiano, *The Black Notebook*, 130.

27. Patrick Modiano, *Dora Bruder*, trans. Joanna Kilmartin (University of California Press, 2015), 73–74.

28. Modiano, *Dora Bruder*, 37.

29. Modiano, *Dora Bruder*, 3–4.

30. Modiano, *Dora Bruder*, 51.

31. Modiano, *Dora Bruder*, 119.

32. Susan Rubin Suleiman, "'Oneself as Another': Identification and Mourning in Dora Bruder," *Studies in 20th & 21st Century Literature* 31, no. 2 (2007): 325–350.

33. Paul Ricœur, *Oneself as Another*, trans. Kathleen Blamey (University of Chicago Press, 1992), 2–4.

34. Ricœur, *Oneself as Another*, 148.

35. Ricœur, *Oneself as Another*, 165.

36. *The Mortified Podcast*, season 1, episode 1, dir. Michael Mayer, Netflix, February 14, 2018.

37. *The Mortified Podcast*, episode 2.

38. *The Mortified Podcast*, episode 2.

39. Renana Raz and Nitzan Cohen, dirs., *Greetings from the Past*, Jerusalem, September 21, 2022.

2. Nonimages

1. Coca-Cola, "Coca-Cola Hungary Advertisement," YouTube video, 0:30, September 2019, https://www.youtube.com/watch?v=HGjWpF-trlg; András Arató, "Waking Up as a Meme-Hero," TEDx Talk, 14:45, TEDxKyiv, June 2019, https://www.youtube.com/watch?v=FScfGU7rQaM; @painharold (András Arató), Instagram, https://www.instagram.com/painharold/.

2. Hito Steyerl, "In Defence of the Poor Image," in *The Wretched of the Screen* (Sternberg, 2012), 32.

3. Steyerl, "In Defence of the Poor Image," 33.

4. Michelle Gorea, "Becoming Your 'Authentic' Self: How Social Media Influences Youth's Visual Transitions," *Social Media & Society* 7, no. 3 (July–September 2021): 1–12, 4.

5. Paul Frosh, "Is Commercial Photography a Public Evil? Beyond the Critique of Stock Photography," in *Photography and Its Publics*, ed. Melissa Miles and Edward Welch (Routledge, 2020), 190–91.

6. Frosh, "Is Commercial Photography a Public Evil?," 192.

7. Frosh, "Is Commercial Photography a Public Evil?," 193.

8. Frosh, "Is Commercial Photography a Public Evil?," 195.

9. Michal Heron, *How to Shoot Stock Photos That Sell* (Allworth, 2001).

10. Heron, *How to Shoot Stock Photos That Sell*, 25.

11. "Ariane—the Overexposed Stock Image Model," Facebook group, https://www.facebook.com/arianefans.

12. Susan Sontag, *On Photography* (Rosetta, 2007), 16.

13. Sontag, *On Photography*, 54.

14. Roland Barthes, *Camera Lucida: Reflections on Photography*, trans. Richard Howard (Vintage, 2000), 5.

15. Barthes, *Camera Lucida*, 41.

16. Barthes, *Camera Lucida*, 96. Italics in the original.

17. Walter Benjamin, "On Some Motifs in Baudelaire," in *Illuminations*, trans. Harry Zohn (Schocken, 1968), 189.

18. Sontag, *On Photography*, 10.

19. Sontag, *On Photography*, 11.

20. Barthes, *Camera Lucida*, 10.

21. Barthes, *Camera Lucida*, 14.

22. Paul Frosh, "The Gestural Image: The Selfie, Photography Theory, and Kinesthetic Sociability," *International Journal of Communication* 9 (2015): 1605.

23. Barthes, *Camera Lucida*, 5.

24. Frosh, "The Gestural Image," 1610.

25. Maria Stepanova, *In Memory of Memory*, trans. Sasha Dugdale (Fitzcarraldo Editions, 2023), 75.

26. Stepanova, *In Memory of Memory*, 76.

27. Stepanova, *In Memory of Memory*, 70.

28. Stepanova, *In Memory of Memory*, 77.

29. Barthes, *Camera Lucida*, 91.

30. Barthes, *Camera Lucida*, 92.

31. Barthes, *Camera Lucida*, 93.

32. Stepanova, *In Memory of Memory*, 79–80.

33. Stepanova, *In Memory of Memory*, 80.

34. Judith Butler, "Gender Is Burning: Questions of Appropriation and Subversion," in *Feminist Film Theory: A Reader*, ed. Sue Thornham (Edinburgh University Press, 1999), 342.

35. Butler, "Gender Is Burning," 343.

36. *Paris Is Burning*, dir. Jennie Livingston (Miramax, 1990).

37. L. V. Anderson, "Vince Vaughn's Stock Photos: Unfinished Business Marketing Move Is Brilliant," *Slate*, March 04, 2015, https://slate.com/culture/2015/03/vince-vaughn-stock-photos-unfinished-business-marketing-move-to-promote-new-movie-is-brilliant.html.

38. Susan Sontag, "Notes on Camp," in *Camp: Queer Aesthetics and the Performing Subject: A Reader*, ed. Fabio Cleto (Edinburgh University Press, 1999), 56.

39. Sontag, "Notes on Camp," 58.

40. Sontag, "Notes on Camp," 60.

41. Andrew Ross, "Uses of Camp," in *Camp: Queer Aesthetics and the Performing Subject: A Reader*, ed. Fabio Cleto (Edinburgh University Press, 1999), 320.

42. ChinnyxD, "Hide the Pain Harold," YouTube video, 3:28, posted September 10, 2014, https://www.youtube.com/watch?v=6eusqf33568.

3. Old Flames

1. Eva Illouz, *The End of Love: A Sociology of Negative Relations* (Oxford University Press, 2019), 17.

2. Illouz, *The End of Love*, 120.

3. Marcel Proust, *In Search of Lost Time: Time Regained*, trans. Andreas Mayor and Terence Kilmartin (Modern Library, 2003), 515.

4. Proust, *Time Regained*, 285.

5. Walter Benjamin, *The Arcades Project*, trans. Howard Eiland and Kevin McLaughlin (Harvard University Press, 1999), 211.

6. Benjamin, *The Arcades Project*, 211.

7. Marcel Proust, *In Search of Lost Time: The Fugitive*, trans. C. K. Scott Moncrieff and Terence Kilmartin (Modern Library, 2003), 578–79.

8. Orhan Pamuk, *The Museum of Innocence*, trans. Maureen Freely (Knopf, 2009), 26.

9. Plato, *Lysis/Symposium/Phaedrus*, ed. and trans. Chris Emlyn-Jones and William Preddy (Harvard University Press, 2022), 205–6.

10. Pamuk, *The Museum of Innocence*, 3.

11. Pamuk, *The Museum of Innocence*, 177.

12. For the story of the museum and its foundation, see Orhan Pamuk, *The Innocence of Objects*, trans. Ekin Oklap (Abrams, 2012).

13. Pamuk admits that staging the stubs at the museum, while writing notes under each one referring to the context in which each one was collected, took him the entire summer of 2011. Pamuk, *The Innocence of Objects*, 228.

14. Pamuk, *The Museum of Innocence*, 156.

15. John Elsner and Roger Cardinal, "Introduction," in *The Cultures of Collecting*, ed. John Elsner and Roger Cardinal (Reaktion, 1994), 3.

16. Krzysztof Pomian, "Collection: une typologie historique," *Romantisme* 112 (2001): 14.

17. Jean Baudrillard, *The System of Objects*, trans. James Benedict (Verso, 1996), 87.

18. Baudrillard, *The System of Objects*, 96–97.

19. Pamuk, *The Museum of Innocence*, 12.

20. Pamuk, *The Museum of Innocence*, 146.

21. Pamuk, *The Museum of Innocence*, 3.

22. Pamuk, *The Museum of Innocence*, 490.

23. Pamuk, *The Museum of Innocence*, 495.

24. Pamuk, *The Museum of Innocence*, 515.

25. Pamuk, *The Museum of Innocence*, 504.

26. Pamuk, *The Museum of Innocence*, 504.

27. Pamuk, *The Museum of Innocence*, 524.

28. Pamuk, *The Museum of Innocence*, 510.

29. Pamuk, *The Museum of Innocence*, 532.

30. *Eternal Sunshine of the Spotless Mind*, dir. Michel Gondry (Universal Pictures, 2004).

31. Alexander Pope, "Eloisa to Abelard," in *The Major Works*, ed. Pat Rogers (Oxford University Press, 2006), 144.

32. Nick Hornby, *High Fidelity* (Penguin, 2021); *High Fidelity*, dir. Stephen Frears (Touchstone Pictures, 2000); *High Fidelity*, season 1, episodes 1–10, created by Veronica West and Sarah Kucserka, aired February 14, 2020, Hulu.

33. Hornby, *High Fidelity*, 31.

34. Hornby, *High Fidelity*, 44.

35. Hornby, *High Fidelity*, 152.

36. Hornby, *High Fidelity*, 188.

37. Hornby, *High Fidelity*, 239.

38. Hornby, *High Fidelity*, 239.

4. Postindustrial Ragpicking

1. Antoine Compagnon, *Les chiffonniers de Paris* (Gallimard, 2017), 12.

2. Compagnon, *Les chiffonniers*, 12.

3. Compagnon, *Les chiffonniers*, 10–14.

4. Charles Baudelaire, *The Flowers of Evil*, trans. James McGowan (Oxford University Press, 2008), 217.

5. Baudelaire, *The Flowers of Evil*, 217.

6. Marc Berdet, *Le chiffonnier de Paris: Walter Benjamin et les fantasmagories* (Vrin, 2015).

7. Berdet, *Le chiffonnier de Paris*, 180.

8. Annie Ernaux, *The Years*, trans. Alison L. Strayer (Seven Stories, 2017), 227.

9. Ernaux, *The Years*, 229.

10. Ernaux, *The Years*, 227.

11. Ernaux, *The Years*, 7–15.

12. Ernaux, *The Years*, 211.

13. Ernaux, *The Years*, 30, 64, 147.

14. Ernaux, *The Years*, 26.
15. Ernaux, *The Years*, 209.
16. Ernaux, *The Years*, 61–62.
17. Ernaux, *The Years*, 212.
18. Ernaux, *The Years*, 209.
19. Ernaux, *The Years*, 209.
20. Ernaux, *The Years*, 214.
21. Ernaux, *The Years*, 213.
22. Annie Ernaux, *A Girl's Story*, trans. Alison L. Strayer (Seven Stories, 2020), 19.
23. Ernaux, *A Girl's Story*, 11, 29.
24. Ernaux, *A Girl's Story*, 35–36.
25. *How To with John Wilson*, season 3, episode 3, "How to Find a Public Restroom," aired August 4, 2023, HBO.
26. Dominique Laporte, *History of Shit*, trans. Nadia Benabid and Rodolphe el-Khoury (MIT Press, 2002), 4.
27. Laporte, *History of Shit*, 30–31.
28. Annie Ernaux, *Exteriors*, trans. Tanya Leslie (Seven Stories, 1996), 6–7.
29. Ernaux, *Exteriors*, 8.
30. Annie Ernaux, *Things Seen*, trans. Jonathan Kaplansky (University of Nebraska Press, 2010), 65.
31. Ernaux, *Exteriors*, 91.
32. Ernaux, *Exteriors*, 91.
33. Ernaux, *Exteriors*, 31.
34. Ernaux, *Exteriors*, 88.
35. Bruce Bégout, *Obsolescence des ruines. Essai philosophique sur les gravats* (Inculte-Dernière Marge, 2022).
36. Roland Barthes, *Mythologies*, trans. Annette Lavers (Farrar, Straus & Giroux, 1972), 97.
37. Barthes, *Mythologies*, 99.
38. Rem Koolhaas, *Delirious New York: A Retroactive Manifesto for Manhattan* (Monacelli, 1994), 9–10.
39. Koolhaas, *Delirious New York*, 10.
40. Koolhaas, *Delirious New York*, 18–21.
41. Koolhaas, *Delirious New York*, 85.

42. Koolhaas, *Delirious New York*, 103.

43. *Redemption*, dir. Jon Alpert and Matthew O'Neill (HBO Documentary Films, 2012).

44. Laporte, *History of Shit*, 17.

45. Laporte, *History of Shit*, 18.

46. Laporte, *History of Shit*, 46.

47. Annie Ernaux, *Look at the Lights, My Love!*, trans. Alison L. Strayer (Yale University Press, 2023), 6.

48. Ernaux, *Look at the Lights*, 4.

49. Ernaux, *Look at the Lights*, 4.

50. Ernaux, *Look at the Lights*, 4.

51. Ernaux, *Look at the Lights*, 32–33.

52. Ernaux, *Look at the Lights*, 25, 79.

53. Ernaux, *Look at the Lights*, 44, 48.

54. Ernaux, *Look at the Lights*, 45.

55. Ernaux, *Look at the Lights*, 80.

5. Childish Profanations

1. Marie Kondo, *The Life-Changing Magic of Tidying*, trans. Cathy Hirano (Ten Speed, 2014), 58.

2. Kondo, *The Life-Changing Magic*, 114.

3. *Tidying Up with Marie Kondo*, season 1, episode 4, "Sparking Joy After a Loss," dir. Jade Sandberg Wallis, aired January 1, 2019, Netflix.

4. *Tidying Up with Marie Kondo*, season 1, episode 6, "Breaking Free from a Mountain of Stuff," dir. Jade Sandberg Wallis, aired January 1, 2019, Netflix.

5. Kondo, *The Life-Changing Magic*, 116–17.

6. Sigmund Freud, "Mourning and Melancholia," in *The Standard Edition of the Complete Psychological Works of Sigmund Freud*, trans. James Strachey (Hogarth, 1953–1974), 14:243–58.

7. Freud, "Mourning and Melancholia," 250–51.

8. George Bataille, *The Accursed Share: An Essay on General Economy*, vol. 1, trans. Robert Hurley (Zone, 1988), 55. Italics in the original.

9. Bataille, *The Accursed Share*, 56. Italics in the original.

10. Giorgio Agamben, "In Praise of Profanation," in *Profanations*, trans. Jeff Fort (Zone, 2007), 81.

11. Agamben, "In Praise of Profanation," 76.

12. *Hoarders*, season 2, episode 2, "Judy and Gail," aired December 7, 2009, A&E.

13. Karl Marx, *Capital: A Critique of Political Economy*, vol. 1, trans. Ben Fowkes (Penguin, 1981).

14. Nicolás Guagnini, "Fetishism/Hoarding/Entropy," in *Materiality*, ed. Petra Lange-Berndt (MIT Press, 2015), 116–17.

15. See a definition of *thingness* in the Introduction.

16. Sigmund Freud, "Civilization and Its Discontents," in *The Standard Edition of the Complete Psychological Works of Sigmund Freud*, trans. James Strachey (Hogarth, 1953–1974), 21:64–145.

17. Harold F. Searles, *The Nonhuman Environment in Normal Development and in Schizophrenia* (International Universities Press, 1960), 102.

18. Searles, *The Nonhuman Environment*, 157.

19. Rebecca R. Falkoff, *Possessed: A Cultural History of Hoarding* (Cornell University Press, 2021), 11.

20. Falkoff, *Possessed*, 7–8.

21. Jane Bennett, "Powers of the Hoard: Further Notes on Material Agency," in *Animal, Vegetable, Mineral: Ethics and Objects*, ed. Jeffrey Jerome Cohen (Punctum, 2012), 248–49.

22. Jane Bennett, *Influx and Efflux: Writing Up with Walt Whitman* (Duke University Press, 2020), 78.

23. Falkoff, *Possessed*, 114.

24. Bennett, "Powers of the Hoard," 243.

25. Bennett, "Powers of the Hoard," 246.

26. Bennett, "Powers of the Hoard," 254.

27. Christopher Bollas, *The Shadow of the Object: Psychoanalysis of the Unthought Known* (Routledge, 2017), 88.

28. Bollas, *The Shadow of the Object*, 88.

29. Bollas, *The Shadow of the Object*, 88.

30. Bollas, *The Shadow of the Object*, 89.

31. Bollas, *The Shadow of the Object*, 91.

32. Searles, *The Nonhuman Environment*, 112.

33. Searles, *The Nonhuman Environment*, 174.

34. Searles, *The Nonhuman Environment*, 175.

35. Bollas, *The Shadow of the Object*, 83.

36. Agamben, "In Praise of Profanation," 83.

37. Giorgio Agamben, *Stanzas: Word and Phantasm in Western Culture*, trans. Roland L. Martinez (University of Minnesota Press, 1993), 59.

38. Giorgio Agamben, "In Playland: Reflections on History and Play," in *Infancy and History: The Destruction of Experience*, trans. Liz Heron (Verso, 1993), 71.

39. Agamben, "In Playland," 71.

40. Agamben, "In Playland," 70.

41. Sigmund Freud, "Beyond the Pleasure Principle," in *The Standard Edition of the Complete Psychological Works of Sigmund Freud*, trans. James Strachey (Hogarth, 1953–1974), 18:15.

42. Freud, "Beyond the Pleasure Principle," 15.

43. Walter Benjamin, "Toys and Play: Marginal Notes on a Monumental Work," trans. Rodney Livingstone, in *Selected Writings*, vol. 2, 1927–1934 (Harvard University Press, 1999), 120.

44. Walter Benjamin, "The Cultural History of Toys," trans. Rodney Livingstone, in *Selected Writings*, vol. 2, 1927–1934 (Harvard University Press, 1999), 115.

45. Michael Powers, "The Smallest Remainder: Benjamin and Freud on Play," *MLN* 133, no. 3 (2018): 730.

46. Powers, "The Smallest Remainder," 732.

47. *Beanie Mania*, dir. Yemisi Brookes (HBO Documentary Films, 2021).

6. Aged Unwell

1. Jean Améry, *On Aging: Revolt and Resignation*, trans. John D. Barlow (Indiana University Press, 1994), 81.

2. Améry, *On Aging*, 102.

3. Améry, *On Aging*, 91.
4. Zygmunt Bauman, *Wasted Lives: Modernity and Its Outcasts* (Polity, 2013), 96.
5. Michel Houellebecq, *Whatever*, trans. Paul Hammond (Serpent's Tail, 2011), 99.
6. Michel Houellebecq, *Serotonin*, trans. Shaun Whiteside (Farrar, Straus & Giroux, 2019), 6–8.
7. Michel Houellebecq, *Submission*, trans. Lorin Stein (Vintage, 2015), 32.
8. Louis Betty, *Without God: Michel Houellebecq and Materialist Horror* (Penn State University Press, 2016), 105, 121.
9. Ben Jeffery, *Anti-Matter: Michel Houellebecq and Depressive Realism* (John Hunt, 2011), 35–36.
10. Douglas Morrey, *Michel Houellebecq: Humanity and Its Aftermath* (Liverpool University Press, 2013), 55–62; Carole Sweeney, *Michel Houellebecq and the Literature of Despair* (A&C Black, 2013), 159.
11. Jean Améry, *On Suicide: A Discourse on Voluntary Death*, trans. John D. Barlow (Indiana University Press, 1999), 27.
12. Michel Houellebecq, *The Map and the Territory*, trans. Gavin Bowd (Knopf, 2012), 5.
13. Houellebecq, *The Map and the Territory*, 17.
14. Houellebecq, *The Map and the Territory*, 18.
15. Houellebecq, *The Map and the Territory*, 18.
16. Houellebecq, *The Map and the Territory*, 51.
17. Houellebecq, *The Map and the Territory*, 59.
18. Houellebecq, *The Map and the Territory*, 54.
19. Houellebecq, *The Map and the Territory*, 167.
20. Houellebecq, *The Map and the Territory*, 138.
21. Houellebecq, *The Map and the Territory*, 104–5.
22. Houellebecq, *The Map and the Territory*, 105.
23. Jean Baudrillard, *Symbolic Exchange and Death*, trans. Iain Hamilton Grant (Sage, 1993), 88.
24. Houellebecq, *The Map and the Territory*, 113.
25. Houellebecq, *The Map and the Territory*, 266.
26. Houellebecq, *The Map and the Territory*, 268.

27. Bauman, *Wasted Lives*, 120.

28. Baudrillard, *Symbolic Exchange and Death*, 146.

29. Baudrillard, *Symbolic Exchange and Death*, 146. Italics in the original.

30. Baudrillard, *Symbolic Exchange and Death*, 163.

31. Houellebecq, *Serotonin*, 136–37.

32. Houellebecq, *Serotonin*, 4.

33. Houellebecq, *Serotonin*, 268.

34. Laurent de Sutter, *Narcocapitalism: Life in the Age of Anaesthesia*, trans. Barnaby Norman (Polity, 2015), 43.

35. de Sutter, *Narcocapitalism*, 43, 107.

36. Houellebecq, *Serotonin*, 1.

37. Houellebecq, *Serotonin*, 154.

38. Houellebecq, *Serotonin*, 51.

39. Houellebecq, *Serotonin*, 206.

40. Houellebecq, *Serotonin*, 308.

41. Peter Conrad, "The E-Cigarette," *21st Century Mythologies*, BBC Radio 4, October 15, 2014, https://www.bbc.co.uk/programmes/b04lozq9.

42. François J. Bonnet, *After Death*, trans. Amy Ireland (MIT Press, 2020), "The Perpetual Present: A Life Sentence."

43. Bonnet, *After Death*, "The Perpetual Present."

44. Houellebecq, *Serotonin*, 306.

45. Houellebecq, *Serotonin*, 291.

7. Better to Burn Out Than to Fade Away

1. "Drowned in the Sun," produced by *Lost Tapes of the 27 Club*, engineered by Over the Bridge using AI, 2021, https://www.losttapesofthe27club.com/.

2. Lev Manovich, "AI Image and Generative Media: Notes on Ongoing Revolution," in *Artificial Aesthetics*, by Lev Manovich and Emanuele Arielli, April 20, 2023, http://manovich.net/index.php/projects/lectures-exhibitions-2015.

3. Simon J. D. Prince, *Understanding Deep Learning* (MIT Press, 2023), 2–5.

4. Arthur I. Miller, *The Artist in the Machine: The World of AI-Powered Creativity* (MIT Press, 2019), 145.

5. Gilles Deleuze, "Literature and Life," in *Essays Critical and Clinical*, trans. Daniel W. Smith and Michael A. Greco (University of Minnesota Press, 1997), 1–6.

6. Gilles Deleuze, *Difference and Repetition*, trans. Paul Patton (Columbia University Press, 1995), 211.

7. Deleuze, *Difference and Repetition*, 211.

8. Deleuze, *Difference and Repetition*, 23.

9. Deleuze, *Difference and Repetition*, 23.

10. Miller, *The Artist in the Machine*, 140.

11. Miller, *The Artist in the Machine*, 141.

12. Miller, *The Artist in the Machine*, 141.

13. Miller, *The Artist in the Machine*, 142.

14. Henri Bergson, *The Creative Mind: An Introduction to Metaphysics*, trans. Mabelle L. Andison (Dover, 2010), 82.

15. Bergson, *The Creative Mind*, 85.

16. Bergson, *The Creative Mind*, 82.

17. Bergson, *The Creative Mind*, 74.

18. Bergson, *The Creative Mind*, 85.

19. Kurt Cobain, *Kurt Cobain Journals* (Penguin, 2002), 87.

20. Cobain, *Journals*, 269.

21. Deleuze, "Literature and Life," 1.

22. Deleuze, "Literature and Life," 1.

23. Gilles Deleuze, *Proust and Signs*, trans. Richard Howard (University of Minnesota Press, 2000), 50–51.

24. Deleuze, *Proust and Signs*, 38.

25. Gilles Deleuze and Félix Guattari, *What Is Philosophy?*, trans. Hugh Tomlinson and Graham Burchell (Columbia University Press, 1994), 168.

26. Deleuze and Guattari, *What Is Philosophy?*, 168.

27. Deleuze and Guattari, *What Is Philosophy?*, 167.

28. Deleuze and Guattari, *What Is Philosophy?*, 168.

29. Quoted in Kieran Curran, *Cynicism in British Post-War Culture: Ignorance, Dust, and Disease* (Palgrave Macmillan, 2015), 188.

30. Curran, *Cynicism in British Post-War Culture*, 188.

31. Peter Szendy, *Hits: Philosophy in the Jukebox*, trans. Will Bishop (Fordham University Press, 2012), 11.

32. Søren Kierkegaard, "Repetition," in *Repetition and Philosophical Crumbs*, trans. M. G. Piety (Oxford University Press, 2009), 3.

33. Kierkegaard, "Repetition," 4.

34. Szendy, *Hits*, 28. Italics in the original.

35. Deleuze, *Difference and Repetition*, 41.

Envoi. Toward Intimate Otherness

1. Jay Rosenblatt, dir., *How Do You Measure a Year?* (Jay Rosenblatt Films, 2022).

2. Callie Holtermann, "Why Are So Many People Rewatching *Girls?*," *New York Times*, March 17, 2023, https://www.nytimes.com/2023/03/16/style/girls-show-hbo-lena-dunham.html.

3. *Girls Rewatch*, podcast hosted by Amelia Ritthaler and Evan Lazarus, independent podcast (2023–), originally on Apple Podcasts/Spotify.

Works Cited

Adorno, Theodor. *Minima Moralia: Reflections from Damaged Life*. Verso, 2005.

Ahmed, Sara. *The Cultural Politics of Emotion*. Edinburgh University Press, 2004.

Agamben, Giorgio. "In Playland: Reflections on History and Play." In *Infancy and History: The Destruction of Experience*, translated by Liz Heron, 65–87. Verso, 1993.

———. "In Praise of Profanation." In *Profanations*, translated by Jeff Fort, 73–92. Zone, 2007.

———. *Stanzas: Word and Phantasm in Western Culture*. Translated by Roland L. Martinez. University of Minnesota Press, 1993.

Améry, Jean. *On Aging: Revolt and Resignation*. Translated by John D. Barlow. Indiana University Press, 1994.

———. *On Suicide: A Discourse on Voluntary Death*. Translated by John D. Barlow. Indiana University Press, 1999.

Anders, Günther. *Die Antiquiertheit des Menschen*. Bd. II: *Über die Zerstörung des Lebens im Zeitalter der dritten industriellen Revolution*. C. H. Beck, 1980.

Anderson, L. V. "Vince Vaughn's Stock Photos: Unfinished Business Marketing Move Is Brilliant." *Slate*, March 4, 2015.

Arató, András. "Waking Up as a Meme-Hero." TEDx Talk, 14:45. TEDxKyiv, June 2019.

Barthes, Roland. *Camera Lucida: Reflections on Photography*. Translated by Richard Howard. Vintage, 2000.

———. *Mythologies*. Translated by Annette Lavers. Farrar, Straus & Giroux, 1972.

Bataille, Georges. *The Accursed Share: An Essay on General Economy*. Vol. 1. Translated by Robert Hurley. Zone, 1988.

Baudelaire, Charles. *The Flowers of Evil*. Translated by James McGowan. Oxford University Press, 1993.

———. *The Painter of Modern Life and Other Essays*. Translated by Jonathan Mayne. Phaidon, 1965.

Baudrillard, Jean. *Symbolic Exchange and Death*. Translated by Iain Hamilton Grant. Sage, 1993.

———. *The System of Objects*. Translated by James Benedict. Verso, 1996.

Bauman, Zygmunt. *Wasted Lives: Modernity and Its Outcasts*. Polity, 2013.

Beanie Mania. Directed by Yemisi Brookes. HBO Documentary Films, 2021.

Bégout, Bruce. *Obsolescence des ruines. Essai philosophique sur les gravats*. Inculte-Dernière Marge, 2022.

Benjamin, Walter. *The Arcades Project*. Translated by Howard Eiland and Kevin McLaughlin. Harvard University Press, 1999.

———. *Berlin Childhood Around 1900*. Translated by Howard Eiland. Harvard University Press, 2006.

———. "The Cultural History of Toys." Translated by Rodney Livingstone. In *Selected Writings*, vol. 2, 1927–1934, 113–16. Harvard University Press, 1999.

———. "On Some Motifs in Baudelaire." In *Illuminations*, translated by Harry Zohn, 155–200. Schocken, 1968.

———. "Paris, the Capital of the Nineteenth Century [1935]." In *The Arcades Project*, translated by Howard Eiland and Kevin McLaughlin, 3–13. Harvard University Press, 1999.

———. "Theses on the Philosophy of History." In *Illuminations*, translated by Harry Zohn, 253–64. Schocken, 1968.

———. "Toys and Play: Marginal Notes on a Monumental Work." Translated by Rodney Livingstone. In *Selected Writings*, vol. 2, 1927–1934, 117–21. Harvard University Press, 1999.

Bennett, Jane. *Influx and Efflux: Writing Up with Walt Whitman*. Duke University Press, 2020.

———. "Powers of the Hoard: Further Notes on Material Agency." In *Animal, Vegetable, Mineral: Ethics and Objects*, edited by Jeffrey Jerome Cohen, 237–69. Punctum, 2012.

Berdet, Marc. *Le chiffonnier de Paris. Walter Benjamin et les fantasmagories*. Vrin, 2015.

Bergson, Henri. *The Creative Mind: An Introduction to Metaphysics*. Translated by Mabelle L. Andison. Dover, 2010.

———. *Matter and Memory*. Translated by Nancy Margaret Paul and W. Scott Palmer. George Allen & Unwin, Humanities Press.

———. "Memory of the Present and False Recognition." In *Key Writings*, edited by Keith Ansell Pearson and John Ó Maoilearca. Bloomsbury, 2002.

Berman, Marshall. *All That Is Solid Melts Into Air: The Experience of Modernity*. Verso, 1983.

Betty, Louis. *Without God: Michel Houellebecq and Materialist Horror*. Penn State University Press, 2016.

Bollas, Christopher. *The Shadow of the Object: Psychoanalysis of the Unthought Known*. Routledge, 2017.

Bonnet, François J. *After Death*. Translated by Amy Ireland. MIT Press, 2020.

Boscagli, Maurizia. *Stuff Theory: Everyday Objects, Radical Materialism*. Bloomsbury, 2014.

Boym, Svetlana. *The Future of Nostalgia*. Basic Books, 2008.

Brown, Bill. "The Obsolescence of the Human." In *Cultures of Obsolescence: History, Materiality, and the Digital Age*, edited by Babette B. Tischleder and Sarah Wasserman, 19–40. Palgrave Macmillan, 2015.

———. *Other Things*. University of Chicago Press, 2020.

Buck-Morss, Susan. "Aesthetics and Anaesthetics: Walter Benjamin's Artwork Essay Reconsidered." *October* 62 (1992): 3–41.

Butler, Judith. "Gender Is Burning: Questions of Appropriation and Subversion." In *Feminist Film Theory: A Reader*, edited by Sue Thornham, 336–49. Edinburgh University Press, 1999.

Chamberlain, Emma. "REACTING TO MY OLD VIDEOS *cringe*." YouTube video. Posted February 9, 2020. https://www.youtube.com/watch?v=McYEPIuz-sI.

ChinnyxD. "Hide The Pain Harold." YouTube video, 3:28. Posted September 10, 2014. https://www.youtube.com/watch?v=6eusqf33568.

Cobain, Kurt. *Kurt Cobain Journals*. Penguin, 2002.

Coca-Cola Hungary Advertisement. YouTube video, 0:30. September 2019. https://www.youtube.com/watch?v=HGjWpF-trlg.

Compagnon, Antoine. *Les chiffonniers de Paris*. Gallimard, 2017.

Conrad, Peter. 2014. "The E-Cigarette." 21st Century Mythologies. BBC Radio 4, October 15. Audio. https://www.bbc.co.uk/programmes/b04lozq9.

Curran, Kieran. *Cynicism in British Post-War Culture: Ignorance, Dust, and Disease*. Palgrave Macmillan, 2015.

Dahl, Melissa. *Cringeworthy: A Theory of Awkwardness*. Portfolio, 2018.

de Sutter, Laurent. *Narcocapitalism: Life in the Age of Anaesthesia*. Translated by Barnaby Norman. Polity, 2015.

Deleuze, Gilles. *Difference and Repetition*. Translated by Paul Patton. Columbia University Press, 1995.

———. "Literature and Life." In *Essays Critical and Clinical*, translated by Daniel W. Smith and Michael A. Greco, 1–6. University of Minnesota Press, 1997.

———. *Proust and Signs*. Translated by Richard Howard. University of Minnesota Press, 2000.

Deleuze, Gilles, and Félix Guattari. *What Is Philosophy?* Translated by Hugh Tomlinson and Graham Burchell. Columbia University Press, 1994.

Derrida, Jacques. "Limited Inc a b c." In *Limited Inc*, translated by Samuel Weber, 29–110. Northwestern University Press, 1988.

———. *Specters of Marx: The State of the Debt, the Work of Mourning, and the New International*. Translated by Peggy Kamuf. Routledge, 1994.

Eichhorn, Kate. *The End of Forgetting: Growing Up with Social Media*. Harvard University Press, 2019.

Elsner, John, and Roger Cardinal, eds. *The Cultures of Collecting*. Reaktion, 1994.

Ernaux, Annie. *Exteriors*. Translated by Tanya Leslie. Seven Stories, 1996.

———. *Look at the Lights, My Love!* Translated by Alison L. Strayer. Yale University Press, 2023.

———. *Things Seen*. Translated by Jonathan Kaplansky. University of Nebraska Press, 2010.

———. *The Years*. Translated by Alison L. Strayer. Seven Stories, 2017.

Eternal Sunshine of the Spotless Mind. Directed by Michel Gondry. 2004. Universal Pictures.

Falkoff, Rebecca R. *Possessed: A Cultural History of Hoarding*. Cornell University Press, 2021.

Freud, Sigmund. "Beyond the Pleasure Principle." In *The Standard Edition of the Complete Psychological Works of Sigmund Freud*, translated by James Strachey, 18:7–64. Hogarth, 1953–1974.

———. "Civilization and Its Discontents." In *The Standard Edition of the Complete Psychological Works of Sigmund Freud*, translated by James Strachey, 21:64–145. Hogarth, 1953–1974.

———. "Mourning and Melancholia." In *The Standard Edition of the Complete Psychological Works of Sigmund Freud*, translated by James Strachey, 14:243–58. Hogarth, 1953–1974.

Frosh, Paul. "The Gestural Image: The Selfie, Photography Theory, and Kinesthetic Sociability." *International Journal of Communication* 9 (2015): 1607–28.

Fukuyama, Francis. *The End of History and the Last Man*. The Free Press, 1992.

Girls Rewatch. Podcast. Hosted by Amelia Ritthaler and Evan Lazarus. 2023–.

Glyman, Alex, and Sara Rankin. "Blurred Lines: Homelessness and the Increasing Privatization of Public Space." Seattle University School of Law, Homeless Rights Advocacy Project, 2016.

Gorea, Michelle. "Becoming Your 'Authentic' Self: How Social Media Influences Youth's Visual Transitions." *Social Media & Society* 7, no. 3 (July–September 2021): 1–12.

Greetings from the Past. Directed by Renana Raz and Nitzan Cohen. Jerusalem, September 21, 2022.

Guagnini, Nicolás. "Fetishism/Hoarding/Entropy." In *Materiality*, edited by Petra Lange-Berndt, 116–19. MIT Press, 2015.

Hartog, François. *Regimes of Historicity: Presentism and Experiences of Time*. Translated by Saskia Brown. Columbia University Press, 2015.

Hartog, François, and Marcin Rychter. "Presentism and Beyond." *Eidos: A Journal for Philosophy of Culture* 4, no. 1 (2020): 110–16.

Hawkins, Gay. "Plastic and Presentism: The Time of Disposability." *Journal of Contemporary Archaeology* 5, no. 1 (2018): 91–102.

Heron, Michal. *How to Shoot Stock Photos That Sell*. Allworth, 2001.

High Fidelity. Created by Veronica West and Sarah Kucserka. Featuring Zoë Kravitz. February 14, 2020. Hulu.

High Fidelity. Directed by Stephen Frears. 2000. Touchstone Pictures.

Hoarders. Season 2, episode 2, "Judy and Gail." Aired December 7, 2009. A&E.

Holtermann, Callie. "Why Are So Many People Rewatching *Girls*?" *New York Times*, March 17, 2023, https://www.nytimes.com/2023/03/16/style/girls-show-hbo-lena-dunham.html.

Hornby, Nick. *High Fidelity*. Penguin, 2021.

Houellebecq, Michel. *The Map and the Territory*. Translated by Gavin Bowd. Knopf, 2012.

———. *Serotonin*. Translated by Shaun Whiteside. Farrar, Straus & Giroux, 2019.

———. *Submission*. Translated by Lorin Stein. Vintage, 2015.
———. *Whatever*. Translated by Paul Hammond. Serpent's Tail, 2011.
How To with John Wilson. Season 3, episode 3, "How to Find a Public Restroom." Created by John Wilson. Aired August 4, 2023. HBO.
Illouz, Eva. *The End of Love: A Sociology of Negative Relations*. Oxford University Press, 2019.
Jeffery, Ben. *Anti-Matter: Michel Houellebecq and Depressive Realism*. John Hunt, 2011.
Kallmekris. "My Old Content Was So CRINGE … " YouTube video. Posted June 2025. https://www.youtube.com/watch?v=eCcsnGoAmzM.
Kierkegaard, Søren. "Repetition." In *Repetition and Philosophical Crumbs*, translated by M. G. Piety, 1–82. Oxford University Press, 2009.
Koenig, Eric. *The Dictionary of Obscure Sorrows*. Simon & Schuster, 2021.
Kondo, Marie. *The Life-Changing Magic of Tidying*. Vermilion, 2014.
———. *Tidying Up with Marie Kondo*. Episode 4, "Sparking Joy After a Loss." Directed by Jade Sandberg Wallis. Aired January 1, 2019. Netflix.
———. *Tidying Up with Marie Kondo*. Episode 6, "Breaking Free from a Mountain of Stuff." Directed by Jade Sandberg Wallis. Aired January 1, 2019. Netflix.
Koolhaas, Rem. *Delirious New York: A Retroactive Manifesto for Manhattan*. Monacelli, 1994.
———. "Junkspace." *October* 100 (2002): 175–90.
Kornbluh, Anna. *Immediacy: Or, the Style of Too Late Capitalism*. Verso, 2024.
Kristeva, Julia. *Powers of Horror: An Essay on Abjection*. Translated by Leon S. Roudiez. Columbia University Press, 1982.
Laporte, Dominique. *History of Shit*. Translated by Nadia Benabid and Rodolphe el-Khoury. MIT Press, 2002.

London, Bernard. *Ending the Depression Through Planned Obsolescence*. Prabhat Prakshan, 2024.

Manovich, Lev. "AI Image and Generative Media: Notes on Ongoing Revolution." In *Artificial Aesthetics*, by Lev Manovich and Emanuele Arielli. April 20, 2023.

Marx, Karl. *Capital: A Critique of Political Economy*. Vol. 1. Translated by Ben Fowkes. Penguin, 1981.

Miller, Arthur I. *The Artist in the Machine: The World of AI-Powered Creativity*. MIT Press, 2019.

Modiano, Patrick. *The Black Notebook*. Translated by Mark Polizzotti. Mariner, 2016.

———. *Dora Bruder*. Translated by Joanna Kilmartin. University of California Press, 2015.

Morrey, Douglas. *Michel Houellebecq: Humanity and Its Aftermath*. Liverpool University Press, 2013.

The Mortified Guide. Season 1. Directed by Michael Mayer. February 14, 2018. Netflix.

Orlando, Francesco. *Obsolete Objects in the Literary Imagination: Ruins, Relics, Rarities, Rubbish, Uninhabited Places, and Hidden Treasures*. Translated by Gabriel Pihas and Daniel Seidel. Yale University Press, 2008.

Pamuk, Orhan. *The Innocence of Objects*. Translated by Ekin Oklap. Abrams, 2012.

———. *The Museum of Innocence*. Translated by Maureen Freely. Knopf, 2009.

Paris Is Burning. Directed by Jennie Livingston. Miramax, 1990.

Plato. *Lysis/Symposium/Phaedrus*. Edited and translated by Chris Emlyn-Jones and William Preddy. Harvard University Press, 2022.

Pomian, Krzysztof. "Collection: une typologie historique." *Romantisme* 112 (2001): 9–22.

Pope, Alexander. "Eloisa to Abelard." In *The Major Works*, edited by Pat Rogers, 137–47. Oxford University Press, 2006.

Powers, Michael. "The Smallest Remainder: Benjamin and Freud on Play." *MLN* 133, no. 3 (2018): 720–42.

Prince, Simon J. D. *Understanding Deep Learning*. MIT Press, 2023.

Proust, Marcel. *In Search of Lost Time: Swann's Way*. Translated by C. K. Scott Moncrieff and Terence Kilmartin, revised by D. J. Enright. Modern Library, 2003.

———. *In Search of Lost Time: The Fugitive*. Translated by C. K. Scott Moncrieff and Terence Kilmartin. Modern Library, 2003.

———. *In Search of Lost Time: Time Regained*. Translated by Andreas Mayor and Terence Kilmartin. Modern Library, 2003.

REACT. "Kids & Teens React to Kids React to Donald Trump (4 Years Later)." YouTube video, approx. 6:00. Posted October 28, 2020. https://www.youtube.com/watch?v=yTYyJTTIXEY.

———. "Kids React to Fax Machines." YouTube video, 5:06. Posted September 17, 2021. https://www.youtube.com/watch?v=9P7hGBoi4Vo.

———. "Kids React to 2000s Hip Hop Legend Missy Elliott (Work . . .)." YouTube video, 11:12. Posted June 25, 2019. https://www.youtube.com/watch?v=8kJyRG1hAhE.

Redemption. Directed by Jon Alpert and Matthew O'Neill. HBO Documentary Films, 2012.

Richter, Gerhard. *Afterness: Figures of Following in Modern Thought and Aesthetics*. Columbia University Press, 2011.

Ricœur, Paul. *Oneself as Another*. Translated by Kathleen Blamey. University of Chicago Press, 1992.

Rosenblatt, Jay. *How Do You Measure a Year?* 28 min. Jay Rosenblatt Films, 2022.

Ross, Andrew. "Uses of Camp." In *Camp: Queer Aesthetics and the Performing Subject: A Reader*, edited by Fabio Cleto, 308–29. Edinburgh University Press, 1999.

Searles, Harold F. *The Nonhuman Environment in Normal Development and in Schizophrenia*. International Universities Press, 1960.

Slade, Giles. *Made to Break: Technology and Obsolescence in America*. Harvard University Press, 2007.

Sontag, Susan. *On Photography*. Rosetta, 2007.

———. "Notes on Camp." In *Camp: Queer Aesthetics and the Performing Subject: A Reader*, edited by Fabio Cleto, 56–65. Edinburgh University Press, 1999.

Stepanova, Maria. *In Memory of Memory*. Translated by Sasha Dugdale. Fitzcarraldo Editions, 2021.

Steyerl, Hito. "In Defence of the Poor Image." In *The Wretched of the Screen*, 31–45. Sternberg, 2012.

Suleiman, Susan Rubin. "'Oneself as Another': Identification and Mourning in Dora Bruder." *Studies in 20th & 21st Century Literature* 31, no. 2 (2007): 325–50.

Sweeney, Carole. *Michel Houellebecq and the Literature of Despair*. A&C Black, 2013.

Szendy, Peter. *Hits: Philosophy in the Jukebox*. Translated by Will Bishop. Fordham University Press, 2012.

Szondi, Peter. "Hope in the Past: On Walter Benjamin." Translated by Harvey Mendelsohn. *Critical Inquiry* 4, no. 3 (1978): 491–506.

Thompson, Michael. *Rubbish Theory: The Creation and Destruction of Value*. Pluto, 2017.

Tischleder, Babette, and Sarah Wasserman, eds. *Cultures of Obsolescence: History, Materiality, and the Digital Age*. New York: Springer, 2015.

United Nations Environment Programme. "Our Planet Is Choking on Plastic." April 4, 2024.

Wasserman, Sarah. *The Death of Things: Ephemera and the American Novel*. University of Minnesota Press, 2020.

Winn, Lance. "Passages: From Arcade to Virtual Arcadia." In *Shopping: Material Culture Perspectives*, edited by Deborah C. Andrews, 73–88. University of Delaware Press, 2016.

Index

Gai Farchi is Minerva Postdoctoral Fellow in the Department of Cultural Semiotics at the University of Potsdam.